FAST-FIX
GI
DIET

hamlyn

FAST-FIX
GI
DIET

Helen Foster

Have a beautiful body in just 14 days the low-GI way!

Notes

It is advisable to check with your doctor before embarking on any exercise or diet plan. The advice given in this book should not be considered a replacement for professional medical treatment. While the information given here is believed to be accurate and the step-by-step instructions have been devised to avoid strain, neither the author nor the publisher can accept any legal responsibility to any injury or illness sustained while following the exercises and diet plan.

Both metric and imperial measurements are given for the recipes. Use one set of measures only, not a mixture of both.

Ovens should be preheated to the specified temperature. If using a fan-assisted oven, follow the manufacturer's instructions for adjusting the time and temperature. Grills should also be preheated.

This book includes dishes made with nuts and nut derivatives. It is advisable for those with known allergic reactions to nuts and nut derivatives and those who may be potentially vulnerable to these allergies, such as pregnant and nursing mothers, invalids, the elderly, babies and children, to avoid dishes made with nuts and nut oils. It is also prudent to check the labels of preprepared ingredients for the possible inclusion of nut derivatives.

The Department of Health advises that eggs should not be consumed raw. It is prudent for more vulnerable people such as pregnant and nursing mothers, invalids, the elderly, babies and young children to avoid uncooked or lightly cooked dishes made with eggs.

Meat and poultry should be cooked thoroughly. To test if poultry is cooked, pierce the flesh through the thickest part with a skewer or fork – the juices should run clear, never pink or red.

All the recipes in this book have been analysed by a professional nutritionist. The analysis refers to each portion without serving suggestions.

First published in Great Britain in 2006 by
Hamlyn, a division of Octopus Publishing Group Ltd
2–4 Heron Quays, London E14 4JP

Copyright © Octopus Publishing Group Ltd 2006

ISBN-13: 978-0-600-61456-2
ISBN-10: 0-600-61456-5

A CIP catalogue record for this book is available from the British Library

Printed and bound in Spain

10 9 8 7 6 5 4 3 2 1

contents

Introduction

one of the most frustrating things about weight loss is that generally you have to make a choice.

Do you follow one of the faddy diets that cut out entire food groups and come with some worrying side-effects but trigger weight loss quickly enough that every time you step on the scales you smile? Or do you go the sensible route, choosing a healthy eating plan where no food is banned, but weight loss is slow and steady? The latter option is great for long-term results, but not so helpful if you're going on holiday in two weeks' time, have a special occasion to go to (and a special outfit to get into) or simply want a motivating burst to kick-start your way on to a longer term weight-loss programme. Picking up this book is the first step towards ending that frustration because you won't have to make those choices. For the first time you can eat a healthy, sensible diet with no faddy foods, no starvation and plenty of healthy fruit, vegetables and wholegrains, and still get results that make you smile when you stand on the scales.

The reason this diet works is that you follow a low-calorie eating plan based on the sound scientific principles of the Glycaemic Index (GI) to trigger steady, safe, sustainable fat loss from your body. In addition, you incorporate some simple toning and cardiovascular exercise to increase that fat loss through aerobic calorie-burning. But things don't end there – this plan also uses daily power-ups that help promote extra weight loss by fighting problems such as a sluggish metabolism, excess fluid and poor posture, which can undermine your weight-loss efforts. The result is that in the 14 days on which you follow this diet you can shed up to 3 kg (6½ lb) – and lose inches from your hips, tummy and thighs.

However, there are more benefits to this diet than weight loss alone. The Glycaemic Index is one of the most exciting areas of nutritional science today. All over the world researchers are investigating the positive health benefits of this simple eating approach and are concluding that eating primarily foods with a low GI can positively influence the health and well-being of every cell in your body. By balancing levels of vital blood sugars, fats and hormones through eating the low-GI way, you create the ideal biological conditions in your body for higher energy levels, positive emotional sensations and all-round general health and longevity.

It's no surprise, therefore, that so many people who start on a low-GI plan (even a short one like this) want to follow its principles for life. And that's where the final benefit of this fast-fix plan reveals itself. While many diet plans – particularly those of the rapid-results variety – leave you high and dry when the plan is over, on this diet you'll learn everything you need to help you continue to follow this healthy way for life.

The result? The next 14 days could be the most important of your life so far for your health.

What is GI?

GI is possibly the most important term you need to know about if you want to lose weight today. It stands for Glycaemic Index and, put very simply, it's a measure of how fast a food turns to the sugar known as glucose (which you use as fuel) in your body. A food that converts quickly is known as a high-GI food, while one that converts slowly is known as a low-GI food.

Admittedly, it's not a new concept – the Glycaemic Index (GI) has been known about for more than two decades (primarily as a way to help diabetics control their insulin levels) – but only recently has the role of GI in weight loss been explored extensively enough to determine its importance.

In the last few years, studies have discovered that:

1 Switching from high-GI foods to low-GI alternatives actually revs up your metabolic rate, increasing the number of calories that you burn each day by 4 per cent, and this alone could see the average woman losing around 3.6 kg (8 lb) a year and the average man losing around 4.7 kg (10½ lb) a year with no further alterations to their diet. But, more importantly for dieters, this metabolic boost dramatically reduces the normal slowdown that occurs when you cut your calorie intake.

2 Low-GI foods also boost fat-burning. According to a study published in the journal *Nutrition and Metabolism*, the presence of the low-GI form of starch (known

than the white-bread eaters. And it's believed that switching to an overall low-GI diet could have an even greater effect.

4 When you switch to eating the low-GI way, your appetite naturally decreases, making weight loss easier than it's ever been before. In a trial proving the metabolic boost of GI eating, researchers also discovered that the dieters felt considerably less hungry than those who were not eating the low-GI way. This echoes past research, which found that the appetite was naturally kept in check on a low-GI diet – in fact, after eating a low-GI meal, volunteers in a trial at Tufts University in Boston, US, consumed 81 per cent fewer calories at their next meal without noticing, thereby dramatically boosting their weight-loss efforts.

5 Eating low-GI foods makes exercise feel easier. Exercise is a vital part of weight loss, and eating the low-GI way actually aids exercise. In a trial undertaken by Case Western University in Ohio, US, women given a low-GI meal before they worked out managed to last 16 per cent longer in exercise tests than high-GI eaters, because they had much more energy with which to sustain their efforts.

Because of these factors many nutritionists now believe that eating the low-GI way is the healthiest – and, potentially, the most effective – way to lose weight and to keep it off for life. But to understand how to do this properly, you need to know exactly how food acts in your body and what makes a food high-GI or low-GI.

as amylose) in your diet actually triggers fat-burning after eating – and it can, in high enough quantities, rev up the speed at which you do this by 23 per cent. Eating a low-GI meal before exercise has also been shown to increase the amount of fat that you burn during your workout.

3 People who switch even just the white bread in their diet to a lower GI alternative gain roughly one-third fewer centimetres (or inches) around their waist every single year than those who eat higher GI white breads, says US-based GI researcher Dr Katherine Tucker in the *American Journal of Clinical Nutrition*. One reason for this could be that the low-GI eaters produce less insulin (which just loves to store excess calories around the abdomen)

GI explained

When you eat a food that contains carbohydrate, that food is converted by your body into a sugar called glucose, which your body uses as energy. The faster a food makes this conversion, the faster sugar enters your system. If you're an athlete who suddenly needs to replenish his or her sugar stores, this is a good thing; however, if you're a sedentary office worker, a sudden rise in glucose levels might not be so positive.

The reason is that if too much glucose is released into your system in one go, your body panics. The result is a rapid release of another hormone, known as insulin, which then shuttles the extra sugar out of your system and into the fat stores. This alone contributes to weight gain – particularly around the abdominal area, where, as mentioned on page 9, insulin has a particular fondness for depositing extra sugar. But to compound the problem, this initial reaction triggers a knock-on nutritional effect.

You see, after insulin has done its job, blood-sugar levels in the body are left low – often too low to provide your organs, muscles and brain with all the fuel they need to carry out the myriad tasks demanded of them every hour. This lack of fuel then causes a different type of panic, which sees the appetite part of the brain sending out strong psychological signals for foods that can help it replenish its fuel stores quickly: psychological signals that you interpret as cravings for chocolate, sweets or easily digested carbohydrates such as white bread and sugary drinks. The result: you eat more high-GI foods and the fat-making circle begins again.

However, switching to low-GI foods stops this vicious circle in its tracks. Low-GI foods convert far more steadily to sugar, eliminating the body's need for a panic reaction and the subsequent sugar cravings to reverse it. The result is that less glucose ends up in your fat stores – and fewer calories end up being consumed to boost your flagging energy levels. These two effects combine to help keep your weight stable. Add calorie control, a little exercise and some fluid-fighting to the mix (as you're going to do in the 14-day diet plan on pages 24–85) and you have an all-round recipe for weight loss.

High GI and low GI

Remember, the GI of a food is determined by how fast the amount of carbohydrate in that food converts to sugar within the body. Because of this, foods that don't contain any carbohydrate – such as meat, fish and poultry (which are pure protein foods) and butter, margarine and cooking oils (which are pure fat) – are automatically assumed to be low-GI foods.

Having a high level of either protein or fat also dramatically lowers GI, which is why beans, pulses, nuts, seeds and dairy products that combine high levels of protein or fat with carbohydrates are generally very low-GI foods. However, within carbohydrate foods, GI values can vary widely, and there are two main factors that influence this variation.

the type of sugar that a food contains

A food that contains a high level of glucose (found in manufactured items such as sports drinks and energy sweets, and also in naturally sweet fruits like watermelon) will convert very quickly to sugar in the body. Other types of sugar convert more slowly. One reason for this is that many sugars (known as disaccharides) are made up of two molecules (one of glucose, one of fructose), which means they have to be split before they can be effectively converted, thereby considerably slowing the time that the process takes. The disaccharide sugars include sucrose (commonly known as table sugar), lactose (the sugar in dairy products) and maltose (which tends to be used as a flavouring in foods). Fructose (the main sugar in fruit) has only one molecule, but because this has to be changed into glucose before it can be used, it, too, has a low GI.

how easy the food is for your body to break down

Fibre is hard for the body to digest, and so the higher the fibre content of a food, the lower

its GI is likely to be. For example, granary bread (which contains fragments of wheat still with the husks on) takes far more effort to break down than white bread (from which the fibrous husks have been removed). However, the other elements that affect GI are the type and form of starch it contains. The more resistant to breakdown the starch in a food is, the lower the GI of that food will be. This explains why rice (which doesn't contain much resistant starch) is never a low-GI food, and why pasta (which contains lots of resistant starch) is always low-GI. But it also explains why so many of us eat high-GI diets most of the time. You see, when you process a food, you make the starch particles within it much smaller, making them easier to break down – and allowing faster conversion to glucose. This explains why white bread has a higher GI than wholemeal bread, and why bran flakes (where the fibrous shell of the bran is crushed while they are shaped) have a higher GI than noodle-shaped bran cereals (which aren't as 'squashed').

GI at a glance

To measure a food's GI scientists evaluate how fast it converts to sugar compared to glucose. If glucose is 100 on the scale, then any food that converts 70 per cent as fast (and above) is said to be a high-GI food; those foods that convert 56–69 per cent as fast are medium-GI foods; and those that convert 55 per cent (and below) as fast are known as low-GI foods. You'll find the ratings for hundreds of foods in the chart on pages 110–125. Some ratings of common foods include:

High GI foods
- Glucose drinks
- White and wholemeal bread
- White rice and quick-cook rice
- Mashed potatoes and jacket potatoes
- Watermelon
- Parsnips
- Dates

Medium GI foods
- Sucrose (ordinary table sugar, which is used in all sorts of cakes, sweets, pastries and soft drinks)
- Basmati rice and brown rice
- Pineapple
- Beetroot
- Carrots
- Crumpets
- Pitta bread
- Pancakes
- Most canned fruits
- Dried figs

Low GI foods
- Oats
- Pasta
- Beans (except broad beans)
- Pulses
- Nuts and seeds
- Grain breads and seeded breads
- Sweet potatoes
- New potatoes
- Apples
- Cherries and berries
- Milk
- Yogurt
- Soya foods, such as tofu, tempeh and yogurt

The best low-GI foods

One of the reasons many experts believe so strongly in the health-boosting powers of the GI diet is because it invariably contains high levels of nutrient-packed fruits, vegetables and wholegrains. Simply following any low-GI diet will help improve your health for this reason, but there are some low-GI foods that deserve inclusion weekly (if not daily) in your diet plans.

1 berries
Blueberries contain the highest levels of antioxidants (substances that neutralize harmful molecules called free radicals). However, all berries are important health-boosters – raspberries and strawberries, for example, contain vital cancer-fighting chemicals.

2 beans and pulses
Studies have shown that diets rich in beans and pulses (which are high in fibre and protein) play an active part in lowering cholesterol and blood pressure and reducing the incidence of diabetes. Eating just four servings a week is believed to cut the risk of heart disease by 22 per cent.

3 cruciferous vegetables
The vegetables in this family (which include broccoli, cabbage, sprouts and cauliflower) all contain a vital cancer-prevention agent called sulforaphane. New research has revealed that steaming vegetables releases more of this agent than boiling, so steam don't boil!

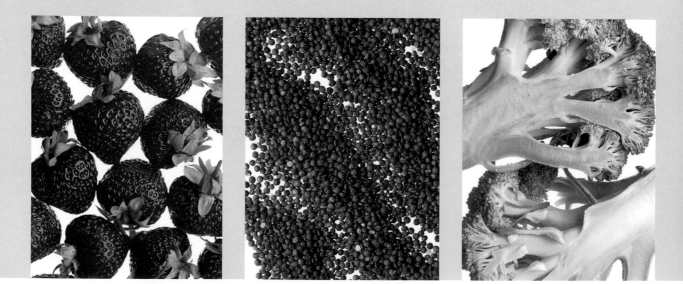

4 dark chocolate

Chocolate is a low-GI food because it contains fat, dairy products and sucrose – and it's a healthy food because it contains antioxidants. However, only good-quality dark chocolate fits the bill, so look for brands containing 70–80 per cent cocoa solids, and stick to just four squares at a time (roughly 100 calories).

6 nuts and seeds

The essential fats in nuts and seeds aren't just linked to a lower risk of heart disease (one handful of nuts per day could cut your risk of heart attack by at least 15 per cent). They also create healthy skin, boost your mood and can even help stimulate fat burning in the body. They are calorific, though, so watch portion sizes closely.

8 quinoa

Many nutritionists say that this grain (which you use as you would rice or couscous) is one of the most complete foods there is. A relative of spinach, quinoa is incredibly high in protein and complex carbohydrates – plus it's packed with energy-giving B vitamins and iron.

9 soya foods

A great source of vegetarian protein, soya is also high in ingredients known as isoflavones, which act like oestrogen in the body. This potentially decreases the risk of breast cancer and menopausal problems in women and may protect against prostate cancer in men. Soya also fights heart disease in both genders.

5 herbs and spices

Adding a pinch of rosemary to your food delivers the same antioxidant benefits as eating a handful of berries. And oregano is nine times more potent than rosemary. Spices such as turmeric and cinnamon also have many health benefits, including potentially fighting diabetes.

7 oats

Well known for their ability to lower cholesterol (one bowl of oats a day can cut cholesterol levels by as much as 23 per cent), oats also control blood sugar and contain a potent antioxidant called ferulic acid, which is linked to a lower risk of colon cancer.

10 sweet potatoes

Ranked top of all vegetables for their fibre and vitamin content by the US-based Center for Science in the Public Interest, sweet potatoes are packed with vitamins A and C, iron and copper. You can cook them just as you would normal potatoes: mashed, chipped or roasted.

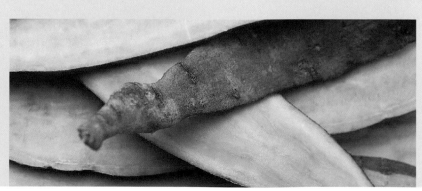

When GI goes bad

Although the list of GI superfoods is beyond reproach, the fact that a high-fat content lowers the GI of a food means that many foods that fit the criteria of healthy in terms of their GI rating have high levels of saturated fat, trans fats and calories. On top of this, other potentially not-so-healthy foods also come with a very low-GI rating. Foods to watch include:

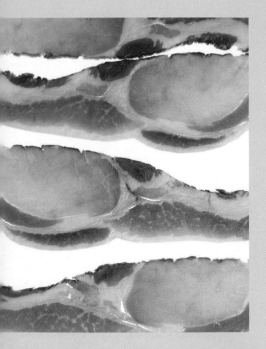

1 bacon, burgers, sausages, etc.
Low-GI because they are packed with protein, these foods do contain high levels of saturated fat, and they are also high in salt, which raises blood pressure and increases the risk of fluid retention. If you want to eat these foods (and other high-fat meats, such as mince and duck), remove any obvious fat before cooking, then grill or dry-fry them; before serving, pat the food with kitchen paper to soak up any surface lipid fats.

2 crisps
Low-GI these may be, but low in calories they are not! If you want something to accompany a sandwich or feel like a snack, you'll get a similar crunch sensation (but many, many more nutrients) if you choose crudités like celery or baby carrots – or try a pickle, such as gherkins or mini onions, which stimulate similar taste receptors to many crisp flavours but with a fraction of the calories.

3 coffee
While coffee doesn't technically raise blood sugar, Dutch researchers have determined that it interferes with the way cells respond to insulin, possibly increasing the amount in your system, which in turn increases the risk of fat storage. Decaffeinated coffee doesn't have this effect, so make the switch today. If you feel that you can't do without that caffeine boost first thing in the morning, at least keep your intake of caffeinated blends down to fewer than four cups a day.

4 diet sodas

While no one has proved that artificial sweeteners are bad for you, researchers at Purdue University in Indiana, US, have found that they do confuse your body's satiety systems, making it more likely that you'll overeat. It's ok to drink diet soda once in a while, but better choices are water, green tea and herbal blends, either drunk hot or cooled and poured over ice.

5 ice cream

Yes, it's delicious, and yes, it contains fat-burning calcium, but ice cream also contains high levels of saturated fat – and the more luxurious the ice cream, the more likely this is. If you want to have an ice-cream dessert once in a while, choose a low-fat variety and serve yourself just one scoop, ideally accompanying it with fruit to boost your nutrient intake and to satiate your appetite.

6 margarine

Many varieties of margarine contain extremely high levels of altered fats known as trans fats, which researchers are now linking to an increased risk of heart disease. Choose varieties that actively say they are trans-fat-free, or use small amounts of butter which may be slightly higher in saturated fat than margarine, but many experts currently believe that this is less harmful than trans fats.

7 spirits

Spirits may be the lowest in GI of any alcoholic drink, but they are also the most potent and are linked to the highest incidence of some digestive cancers and diabetes. Wine may have a slightly higher GI, but if it is drunk as part of a meal or with a small handful of cashews or almonds (which will slow down its sugar conversion), it's a far healthier alcoholic choice.

GI health benefits

With so many healthy foods incorporated into eating the low-GI way, it's easy to see that it's going to be good for your health. However, the benefits could be even greater than you believed.

GI fights major illnesses

As we explained on pages 8–9, one of the main problems of a high-GI diet is that it increases the levels of insulin in your body. And this isn't just bad news for your waistline – insulin can be a very harmful substance. Not only is it linked to a higher incidence of diabetes, but high insulin levels also encourage the production of hormones that can promote growth in some cancer cells, with the result that breast and pancreatic cancers have both been linked to high-GI diets. But lowered insulin isn't the only consequence of cutting down on high-GI foods. Studies have also shown that cutting down on refined foods reduces the levels of cholesterol and heart-disease-triggering fats called triglycerides. Finally, researchers in Seoul, South Korea, have discovered that simply swapping one high-GI food for a lower GI equivalent (in this case white rice for other wholegrains) reduced levels of the harmful amino acid known as homocysteine. This is incredibly important, because this particular amino acid is known to be linked to heart problems and is believed to be a major contributor to the debilitating condition, Alzheimer's disease.

GI fights minor health problems

By tackling blood-sugar swings, low-GI eating is known to help reduce the effects of pre-menstrual syndrome. It's also linked to a greater control of hormones in general, which could help reduce the risk of a condition called polycystic ovary syndrome as well as other fertility problems. However, a more general benefit is that eating the low-GI way may boost your immune system. When you eat a low-GI diet, the amount of sugar in your body is naturally reduced – which is good news, because sugar is an immune-suppressor. Eating the low-GI way also increases the amount of vitamin C that you are able to absorb from

skin. More importantly, high insulin levels in the body have been linked to increased rates of acne and oily skin – and, possibly, to a faster rate of ageing. By reducing the levels of insulin in your diet you'll be helping to create healthy skin from within. And because protein foods feature heavily in low-GI diets, your hair will thank you, too. Hair is made from protein, but if you're not getting enough protein in your diet, your hair is the area to which your body will limit supplies. By boosting your protein intake to adequate levels, you could find that in a matter of weeks your hair both looks shinier and feels healthier and thicker.

foods (because vitamin C and glucose compete to enter the body's cells), and it's well known that people with high blood levels of vitamin C are less susceptible to minor ailments such as colds and flu than those with lower levels.

GI boosts your mood and energy

By providing your body with a slow, steady supply of energy, you prevent the peaks and troughs that trigger the mood and energy swings that many people experience throughout the day. In fact, within two or three days of starting to eat the low-GI way you should find that your energy levels improve. In addition to this, you'll also possibly be eating higher levels of carbohydrate foods on this diet plan than you would normally do while slimming, and this is important as it boosts levels in the brain of the mood-enhancing hormone serotonin. Low levels of serotonin have been linked to depression and comfort-eating.

GI enhances your looks

By adding high levels of essential fats (in the form of nuts and seeds) to your diet, you immediately enhance the appearance and health of your

The GI pyramid

Now that you've seen all the positive effects of eating the low-GI way, you're probably wondering what on earth you should be eating (and when) to harness those benefits. Well, the diagram opposite explains everything quickly and simply. It's called the GI pyramid, and it's been designed to show, at a glance, what makes up a healthy low-GI diet.

There are seven layers overall: foods with a high GI (which also contain few additional nutrients) are shown at the top of the pyramid, while foods with a low GI (but high nutrient values) appear at the bottom. Not surprisingly, foods at the top of the pyramid should be severely limited, while several portions of those foods at the bottom should be eaten every day.

foods at the top of the pyramid

These foods don't just have a high GI; they also contain few additional nutrients or lots of fat. They include glucose drinks, sugary drinks, such as soda, boiled sweets and similar treats, crisps, cakes, biscuits, pastries and sugary puddings. If you eat these at all, make it no more than once a week.

second-layer foods

These include mashed potatoes, white and brown breads, rice and sugar cereals. They're still very high-GI foods, but they do have some nutrients in them, so they're not totally banned. Restrict servings to one or two a week, though – and always eat them with a low-GI food, which slows down the speed at which they convert to sugar.

third-layer foods

Nuts and seeds have a low GI. They are also a good source of fibre and oils, containing essential fatty acids, so you should aim to have 25 g (1 oz) of these each day. You can also include nut- or seed-based products in this category, which means foods like peanut butter and spreads like tahini (made from sesame seeds). Roughly 1½ teaspoons of these products will contain the same number of calories as 25 g (1 oz) of nuts or seeds.

fourth-layer foods

These are the pure protein foods, such as red meats (beef, pork and lamb), poultry (chicken, turkey, duck and goose), offal (kidneys, heart and liver), fish (white fish such as cod and plaice, and oily fish such as salmon, herrings, sardines, pilchards, fresh tuna and trout), shellfish (oysters, crab, prawns, winkles, cockles and mussels) and eggs. Because they contain no carbohydrates, they have a GI of 0. Aim for two or three portions of these foods a day.

fifth-layer foods

Their combination of protein and the relatively slow-digesting sugar known as lactose make milk and dairy products low-GI foods. They're also an important source of calcium, which isn't just good for your bones – research has proved that it also helps reduce fat storage. Aim for two to three servings of dairy products a day – but choose low-fat varieties to cut down on calories and saturated fat intake.

sixth-layer foods

These foods are the starchy carbohydrates, which should give you your main source of energy. You should eat between six and eleven servings of carbohydrates a day, focusing mainly on low-GI varieties, such as granary bread, pasta, oats, grains like barley and quinoa, and sweet or new potatoes. However, if you have already eaten any servings of the starchy carbohydrates (such as white bread and rice) that appear higher up the GI pyramid, then you need to reduce the number of helpings of low-GI foods accordingly.

foods at the bottom of the pyramid

It is recommended that everyone eats at least five portions of fruit and vegetables per day, and virtually all fruit and vegetables have a low GI. There are a few exceptions to this (including watermelon and root vegetables, such as pumpkin or swede), but

one of the problems with the GI testing system is that the amount of fruit and vegetables tested is far greater than you would actually eat, meaning that the insulin effect they will actually have in your body is lessened. Because of this, it's now generally agreed that it's okay to eat all fruit and vegetables on a low-GI diet.

Portion distortion

Although choosing low-GI foods naturally puts your body into a positive state for slimming (remember, your metabolic rate is going to be faster than on any other form of dieting programme and you'll be more likely to burn fat by eating the low-GI way), weight loss is always a matter of calories in versus calories out, so portion sizes do count.

The GI pyramid on page 21 indicates the overall proportions of the different food groups that you should eat each day. Now you'll learn how big that portion should actually be, to fit the diet plan that follows.

• **Bread:** 1 slice of a loaf; half a small roll/bagel

• **Breakfast cereal:** 25 g (1 oz) – roughly 3 tablespoons

• **Butter and spreads** – enough to cover the tip of a knife

• **Cheese:** 40 g (1½ oz) – a piece the size of a matchbox

• **Eggs:** one medium-sized egg

• **Fish:** 150 g (5 oz) – the size of a cheque book but slightly thicker

• **Fruit:** one medium piece (such as an apple or orange); two small pieces of fruit, such as kiwi; enough berries to fit in two cupped hands; or one-eighth of a large fruit, such as a watermelon

• **Fruit juice:** 150 ml (¼ pint) – that's roughly three fingers high in a small glass

• **Meat:** 125 g (4 oz) – the size of a pack of playing cards

• **Milk (dairy or soya):** 200 ml (7 fl oz) – that's roughly four fingers high in a small glass

• **Nuts and seeds:** 25 g (1 oz) – enough to fit in the palm of a cupped hand

• **Oils:** ½ tablespoon, but it's better to use an oil spray, which cuts down on the calories

• **Potatoes:** 125 g (4 oz) – that means an egg-sized whole potato, two small boiled potatoes or roughly 2 heaped tablespoons mashed potato

• **Rice, pasta, couscous:** 25 g (1 oz) in dry weight – that's roughly one large serving spoonful when cooked

• **Shellfish:** 150 g (5 oz) – roughly two cupped hands full of prawns, mussels, clams, etc.

• **Vegetables:** enough to fit in two cupped hands

• **Yogurt (dairy or soya) or cottage cheese:** one small pot (normally 125 g/4 oz)

FAST

This 14-day diet plan works because it combines all the weight-loss benefits of eating the low-GI way (increased metabolic rate, greater fat metabolism, reduced sugar cravings and an increase in energy that makes anything seem possible) with simple calorie-burning exercises and power-up tricks. These either make it easier for you to stay motivated or enhance the weight-loss effects of the diet by reducing fluid retention and other problems such as poor posture. After just 14 days on this plan you will notice your changes.

lose weight

The combination of carefully calorie-counted menus, exercise and increased metabolic stimulation guarantees weight loss of up to 3 kg (6½ lb) on this programme. Together with the feel good tips that you will follow each day, this leads to more rapid weight loss than traditional low-GI plans offer, helping you to achieve your fast-fix aims as easily as possible. As a general rule, the more you weigh to start with, the greater your weight loss will be (because you burn more calories from day to day anyway), but everyone who follows the plan as directed will lose weight.

look and feel thinner

A combination of weight loss, better posture and light muscle toning will ensure you start to lose inches around the tummy, hips and thighs. If you really want to track your progress, wrap a piece of string round your waist before the diet starts (either mark with a pen where the two ends meet or snip the string to fit); at the end of the two weeks, try this again – it's almost certain the string will be too big.

improve your skintone

As we have already mentioned on page 19, better skin is a major benefit of eating the low-GI way, and within just two weeks of increasing your daily intake of essential fats, cutting down on sugars and boosting your intake of fluids, you will plump up dehydrated skin on your face and body, giving you a head-to-toe glow.

reduce signs of cellulite

Cellulite is a combination of fat and fluid, and by helping you lose weight and flush out fluid (together with toning exercises that firm the muscles under those lumps and bumps) this diet could help mild cases of cellulite vanish within a fortnight. More serious cases will take longer, but the increased hydration of your skin will definitely make cellulite less noticeable while you concentrate on defeating those stubborn areas for good.

So that's it: a head-to-toe body make-over in just 14 days. Of course, to get results you need to follow the plan as directed, so read on to discover exactly what you need to do and when.

need some extra help?

If you've got more than 3 kg (6½ lb) to lose (or just love the effects of this fast-fix GI diet so much that you want to keep going when the 14 days are over), that's no problem. You can either repeat the diet exactly as it is or chop and change things, using the alternative options suggested with the recipes. For meals where no alternative is given, remember that you can always swap like for like on a diet – so, any fruit can be replaced by another fruit; any vegetable can be swapped for another vegetable; any meat can be swapped for meat, fish or poultry in the same-size portion; and you can swap any carbohydrate for another low-GI carb as well.

What to do and when

The 14-day plan that follows includes three main elements: 'food', 'fit' and 'feel good'. Each is explained in greater detail below, but every day the minimum you should do is eat the meals and snacks suggested and carry out the toning exercises that appear on pages 90–103. The 'fit' and 'feel good' tips will help boost your results, so try and incorporate as many of them as possible.

food

Every day you'll find three main meals and two snacks to eat. This may actually be more food than you're used to eating (especially when you're trying to slim), but don't skip any meal or snack. Eating regularly actually boosts weight loss, by fooling your body into thinking it's eating more than it is, so preventing the metabolic slowdown that usually occurs when you cut calories. You'll notice that each day there is a recipe to follow or an easy-to-make alternative if you don't fancy cooking that day. Don't always choose the easy alternative, though – all the recipes here are quick to make and will stop you feeling

deprived while you slim (one of the main reasons why dieters fall off the wagon). Remember, if you don't like a particular

ingredient, you can swap it for an alternative (see page 25 for further information on how to do this).

feel good

The 'feel good' tips aim either to enhance the weight-loss effects of the diet or, simply, to create a healthier, happier body to show off your new shape. Again, adding a tip each day (or at least two or three times a week) will boost your results and/or your all-round health. You don't have to follow the tips in the order in which they appear; you can try them in whatever order best fits your mood or personal needs.

fit

On pages 90–103 you'll find an easy ten-minute exercise plan to carry out each day. This helps to tone and strengthen your muscles and will enhance the weight-loss effects of the diet. Each day on the 14-day plan you'll also find a suggestion for a 'fit' task. This will help to increase the calories that you burn each day, and you should aim to add at least two of these tasks each week (or, even better, try a new one each day). Remember, the amount of weight you lose on any diet is determined by the difference between the number of calories you eat and the number you burn off. You'll find some extra exercise suggestions on pages 104–107. To really boost results, aim for 30–60 minutes of any of these at least two or three times a week.

socializing on the plan

One of the biggest problems when following a diet is that life can often get in the way. Eating out or having friends round for dinner may appear to be difficult, but as long as you stick to some simple rules, it really needn't be a problem.

• Eat low-calorie and low-GI, whatever happens. If you're going out for dinner, stick to two courses and make sensible low-calorie choices. Good starter suggestions are clear soups, smoked salmon or prawn cocktail, chicken tikka or Parma ham with melon. For the main course, choose plain fish, meat or poultry with salad (carbs are best avoided) or a small portion of pasta with a fish or vegetable sauce. Most desserts tend to be high in GI or calories, so skip these if possible or order a small scoop of ice cream or sorbet. It might not be your dream order, but the plan is only for 14 days.

• Avoid alcohol altogether as it increases your appetite and boosts fluid retention.

• If you're cooking for other people, swap the evening meal for one of the more exotic suggestions, such as Lemon and Lime Chicken (page 85), Oriental Gingered Salmon (page 45) or Spicy Beef (page 69). The calorie count may differ slightly from your recommended meal, but it will still be low-GI enough to get results. Afterwards serve a low-calorie dessert, such as the jelly on page 33, or some fresh figs with a little crème fraîche.

Getting started

It's a lot easier to stick to a plan if you've got the ingredients you need for each day in your cupboard. Below you'll find a simple shopping list of things you might need to stock up on before you start the plan. Opposite are the answers to some questions that might be going through your head right now.

diet shopping list

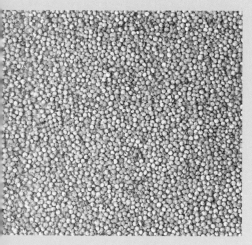

• **Seeds and nuts:** if you find these very moreish, divide them into small handful-sized packs covered with clingfilm.

• **Herbs and spices used in the recipes:** most of these are common herbs like basil or mint, but do check that you have everything you need.

• **Sourdough/soy linseed bread:** you'll find these on the bread counter at large supermarkets or in health-food stores. If you can't find them, granary bread is an alternative.

• **Spelt crisp breads:** these are made of a particularly low-GI type of flour. Again, you'll find them in health-food stores or in the speciality foods section of your local supermarket. Rye crisp breads or oatcakes make good replacements.

• **Canned beans or lentils:** these are a quick-fix alternative to using pulses that need to be soaked before cooking. To determine your portion size, as a general rule, use a weight three times that of the dry weight suggested in any recipe.

• **Grains such as bulgar and quinoa:** these are lower GI alternatives to rice or couscous, and you'll find them in health-food stores or supermarkets. Quinoa is the quickest to cook (taking 15 minutes), while bulgar needs to be soaked for about 30 minutes.

• **Low-GI breakfast cereals,** such as noodle-shaped bran varieties, low-sugar muesli and porridge oats: there are many different recipes on offer for breakfast, but if you're pushed for time in the morning it's ok to start the day with a 25 g (1 oz) serving of cereal (40 g/1½ oz of porridge), topped or made up with 150 ml (¼ pt) skimmed milk and a piece of fruit. Remember, breakfast is the most important meal of the day!

what if I'm vegetarian?

If you're vegetarian there's always an option in the plan for you. In addition, you can adapt any of the recipes by replacing the meat in them with a vegetarian alternative such as tofu, tempeh, Quorn, TVP, beans or pulses or just a selection of vegetables. In most cases this will lower the calorie count as well, so use 50 per cent more than the amount suggested in the recipe to prevent you from eating too little each day.

what if I work all day?

While most of the meal options for lunch can easily be taken to work (or, in many cases, bought from the supermarket or local shop on the day), if you really don't have time to make complicated lunches or have only limited resources near your workplace, here are three simple low-GI lunches that you can eat on any day and know that you won't bust your calorie budget.

• Two slices of granary bread spread with a little mustard and filled with two or three slices of ham, chicken, roast beef, or 2 tablespoons tuna in brine. Add unlimited salad and serve with a small can of slimmer's soup or with three handfuls of baby carrots or celery sticks.

• One small (tennis-ball-sized) jacket potato, topped with 3 tablespoons baked beans. Follow this with a piece of fruit.

• A salad made from a mix of any vegetables you like and topped with three slices of ham, chicken or roast beef, 25 g (1 oz) low-fat cheese, 100 g (3½ oz) low-fat cottage cheese or 50 g(2 oz) tuna and two crispbreads or oatcakes.

what if I eat my main meal at lunch?

Then swap things round — there's no reason why you can't.

what if I'm a night-time nibbler?

This is a major problem for dieters and one of the reasons why each evening meal of this 14-day plan has a suggested dessert. If you know you like to eat at night, don't eat this immediately after your main meal, but wait until your normal 'nibble' time and have it then.

day 1

A new day and a new diet – but this one will be unlike anything you've tried before. There are going to be no hunger pangs, no feelings of deprivation and no sugar cravings to have you searching for chocolate at 3 p.m. This time losing weight is going to feel simple and satisfying.

food

breakfast

glass of apple juice or unsweetened cranberry juice
150 ml (¼ pint)

toast with jam
Spread sugar-reduced jam thinly on 2 slices of toasted sourdough, soy/linseed or granary bread.

ALTERNATIVE
bowl of bran cereal or low-sugar muesli
3 tablespoons cereal with 200 ml (7 fl oz) skimmed milk.

snack

pot of low-fat yogurt with strawberries or raspberries
150 g (5 oz) natural yogurt served with a handful of strawberries or raspberries.

lunch

baked potato, baked beans and salad
Top a large baked potato (250 g/8 oz) with 5 tablespoons baked beans. Serve with a large green salad made with cucumber, lettuce and assorted salad leaves.

ALTERNATIVE
grilled tomatoes and mushrooms
Serve on 2 slices of toasted sourdough, soy/linseed or granary bread.

dessert

apple

snack

handful of peanuts and raisins
25 g (1 oz)

dinner

low-GI vegetable stir-fry
(see page 32)

ALTERNATIVE
grilled gammon steak with vegetables
Grill a 125 g (4 oz) gammon steak and serve with 2 small sweet potatoes, mashed with a little garlic and skimmed milk, and a large portion of mangetout and carrots.

dessert

real strawberry jelly
(see page 33)

fit

Burning calories each day needn't be tricky. Recent research from the Mayo Clinic in the United States revealed that the difference between naturally thin people and those who tend to put on weight is something called the NEAT factor. NEAT stands for Non Exercise Achieved Thermogenesis — and in simple terms it means that the more you walk, stand or fidget each day, the more calories you burn and the thinner you're likely to be.

Up your NEAT factor each day by standing or pacing to make phone calls, by always taking the stairs or walking up the escalator, and by doing all those things your parents told you not to do, such as tapping your fingers or feet as you sit. Remember, every single move you make each day burns calories.

feel good

Each day of the 14-day diet plan you can have 200 ml (7 fl oz) of skimmed or semi-skimmed milk for use in teas and coffees. In addition, you should aim to drink at least 2 litres (3½ pints) of water each day – that's between six and eight glasses. This isn't just to stop you feeling thirsty; when you're dehydrated, your metabolism slows down by as much as 3 per cent, which means you will burn up to 60 fewer calories a day, which adds up to 2.7 kg (6 lb) a year in weight that you could have lost.

To boost your fluid intake, drink either tap or bottled water. If you don't like the taste of water, put a splash of fruit juice or low-sugar cordial or squash in it to flavour it. Or try herbal teas, either drunk hot or mixed in a large jug and cooled in the fridge – this works really well with fruit teas such as blackberry or with a cooling peppermint blend.

Alcohol doesn't count towards your 2 litres (3½ pints) each day as it dehydrates the body, adds calories and reduces your levels of vital fat-burning B vitamins. Caffeine has a similar effect, so try to stick to fewer than four cups of tea or coffee a day, or choose decaffeinated blends.

low-GI vegetable stir-fry

preparation: 10 minutes | **cooking:** 20 minutes | **serves:** 4

1 tablespoon olive oil or rapeseed oil

1 large onion, diced

1 large red pepper, cored, deseeded and diced

2 celery sticks, sliced

2 tablespoons light soy sauce

2 tablespoons tomato ketchup

pinch of chilli powder

125 g (4 oz) mushrooms, trimmed and sliced

10 cherry tomatoes, halved

125 g (4 oz) mangetout or French beans, halved if large

125 g (4 oz) bean sprouts

2 large carrots, cut into batons

4 wholemeal pitta breads, to serve

spring onion curls, to garnish (optional)

1 Heat the oil in a large nonstick pan or wok. Add the onion and cook for 2 minutes.

2 Add the red pepper and celery and sauté for a few minutes. Add the soy sauce, tomato ketchup and chilli powder and stir well.

3 Add the remaining vegetables and stir-fry over a medium heat for 10–15 minutes until the vegetables are tender. Add a small amount of water if necessary.

4 Garnish the stir-fry with spring onion curls, if liked, and accompany each serving with a wholemeal pitta bread.

nutritional values per serving
Kcals **121 (508 kJ)**
Protein **5.5 g**
Carb **17.2 g**
Sodium **44 mg**
Fat **3.8 g**
Sat. fat **0.6 g**
GI **Low**

tip

This recipe can be easily adapted to a different selection of vegetables. If you need to eat it in a hurry, serve in a pitta pocket or a tortilla.

real strawberry jelly

preparation: 5 minutes | **chilling time:** 1–2 hours | **serves:** 4

1 packet (about 13 g ½ oz) sugar-free strawberry jelly

150 g (5 oz) strawberries, hulled, and sliced if large

strawberries, to decorate

low-fat cream, to serve

1 Make up the jelly according to the instructions on the packet.

2 Arrange the strawberries in a mould or basin. Slowly pour the jelly into the mould. Chill for 1–2 hours or until firmly set.

3 To turn out the jelly from a mould, dip the base of the mould in a bowl of hot water for about 10 seconds. Loosen the edge of the jelly with a fingertip and invert a serving plate on top of the mould. Turn upside down and shake firmly – the jelly should be released. If not, re-dip the mould in hot water and repeat. If the jelly is made in a basin, run a knife around the side and then invert on to a plate and shake firmly.

4 Decorate the jelly with more strawberries and serve with a drizzle of low-fat cream.

nutritional values per serving
Kcals **20 (84 kJ)**
Protein **2.2 g**
Carb **2.5 g**
Sodium **71 mg**
Fat **0 g**
Sat. fat **0 g**
GI **Low**

day 2

If you didn't weigh yourself yesterday, get on the scales first thing this morning. Your body's weight-loss systems will already have started to burn fat, while all the extra water you're drinking will ensure that any excess fluid is beginning to be released from your tissues – and you'll want to measure your progress from the outset to get the most motivational results.

food

breakfast

bowl of porridge
Made using 3 tablespoons rolled oats and 200 ml (7 fl oz) water or skimmed milk. Top with a handful of strawberries or raspberries.

ALTERNATIVE
toast and peanut butter
Spread peanut butter on 2 slices of toasted sourdough, soy/linseed or granary bread.

snack

pear

lunch

low-GI lentil and courgette soup
(see page 36)

ALTERNATIVE
bought sandwich
Choose a sandwich made with granary bread and with fewer than 300 kcals.

dessert

slice of melon or handful of berries

snack

pot of low-fat natural fromage frais
150 g (5 oz)

dinner

blackened cod with citrus salsa
(see page 37)

ALTERNATIVE

omelette
Made with 2 eggs and cooked
in a nonstick pan with a minimum
of rapeseed or olive oil. Fill with
mushrooms, onions and
courgettes or 2 slices of lean
ham. Serve with a large green
side salad and a granary roll.

dessert

fresh fruit salad
Made with a selection of fruit,
such as a sliced banana, sliced
Gala apple, orange and grapefruit
segments and strawberries, with
a little added unsweetened
orange juice.

fit

Dancing is a great way to burn
calories – and, because it's fun,
you don't always notice how
long you're 'exercising' for.
Research at Springfield College,
Massachusetts, has discovered
that exercisers work out on
average 27 per cent longer if
they do it to music. So, close the
curtains, put on your favourite
CD and dance around the house
for 30 minutes.

feel good

Stress can affect your waistline.
Not only does feeling under
pressure make it more likely that
you'll comfort-eat, but stress
hormones such as cortisol
actually contribute to fat storage
– especially in the tummy area.
One of the easiest ways to
unwind is in an aromatherapy
bath. Lavender is the most
commonly used aromatherapy
oil, but there are other essential
oils that can help dieters boost
their motivation.

Try making a blend of two drops
of thyme, rosemary and grapefruit
(added to 6 ml/¼ fl oz of carrier
oil) to boost your motivation and
feelings of success; or use two

drops of frankincense plus two
of lavender to give you a great
night's sleep, thereby preventing
fatigue-related nibbles the next
day. So turn on the taps, add your
aromatherapy oil as the bath runs
to enhance the scents, shut the
door and indulge in half an hour
of serenity and calm.

fact

People who follow a low-GI
diet tend to have lower blood
pressure than those who eat
the high-GI way.

low-GI lentil and courgette soup

preparation: 10 minutes | **cooking:** 45 minutes | **serves:** 4

2 vegetable stock cubes

500 ml (17 fl oz) boiling water

50 g (2 oz) lentils

4 courgettes, chopped

4 small onions, chopped

400 g (13 oz) can chopped tomatoes

1 teaspoon chopped fresh mixed herbs

pepper

4 granary rolls, to serve

1 Dissolve the stock cubes in the boiling water in a saucepan. Add the lentils and simmer for 15 minutes.

2 Add all the remaining ingredients to the pan and cook for 30 minutes or until the vegetables are soft

3 Keep the soup chunky by briefly crushing the vegetables with a potato masher. Serve immediately with granary rolls.

tip

This is a really substantial soup and easy to cook. If you have not made soup before it will inspire you to make other soups using a different selection of vegetables. The soup can easily be transported in a flask for a packed lunch.

nutritional values per serving
Kcals **110 (465 kJ)**
Protein **7.0 g**
Carb **18.9 g**
Sodium **633 mg**
Fat **1.5 g**
Sat. fat **0 g**
GI **Low**

blackened cod with citrus salsa

preparation: 10 minutes | **cooking:** 13 minutes | **serves:** 4

1 large orange

1 garlic clove, crushed

2 large tomatoes, deseeded and diced

2 tablespoons chopped basil

50 g (2 oz) black olives, chopped

1 tablespoon extra virgin olive oil

4 cod fillets, about 150 g (5 oz) each

1 tablespoon jerk seasoning

pepper

chopped basil, to garnish

large green salad and 200 g (7 oz) new potatoes, boiled in their skins, to serve

1 Cut the skin and white membrane from the orange. Working over a bowl to catch the juice, cut between the membranes to remove the segments. Halve the segments and mix them with the reserved orange juice, the garlic, tomatoes, basil, olives and half the oil. Season with pepper and set aside to infuse as a salsa.

2 Brush the cod fillets with the remaining oil and coat with the jerk seasoning. Heat a large ovenproof pan and fry the cod fillets, skin side down, for 5 minutes. Turn them over and cook them for a further 3 minutes. Transfer to a preheated oven, 150°C (300°F), Gas Mark 2, for about 5 minutes.

3 Garnish the fish with chopped basil and serve with the salsa, a green salad and new potatoes.

nutritional values per serving
Kcals **216 (904 kJ)**
Protein **28.8 g**
Carb **7.0 g**
Sodium **381 mg**
Fat **8.2 g**
Sat. fat **1.2 g**
GI **Low**

day 3

You should be feeling really positive about this plan now – you've realized how easy it is, after all. But from today you'll start to see some extra benefits. Already your blood-sugar levels will have stabilized dramatically, leaving you bursting with vitality. Say goodbye to 3 p.m. energy slumps and hello to a brighter new you.

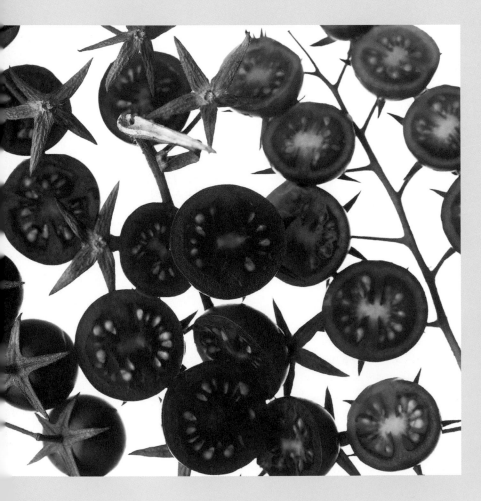

food

breakfast

berry breakfast
(see page 40)

ALTERNATIVE
large pink grapefruit plus 1 slice of toast
toast 1 slice of granary, soy/linseed or sourdough bread and serve with a scraping of low-fat spread

snack

2 seeded crisp breads topped with slices of pear or apple

lunch

it's a wrap
(see page 41)

ALTERNATIVE

salad

Made with lettuce and assorted salad leaves, cucumber, grated carrot, plum tomatoes and radishes together with 40 g (1½ oz) low-fat grated cheese or 50 g (2 oz) lean ham. Serve with a slice of soy and linseed bread.

dessert

banana

snack

low-fat chocolate mousse
Small tub (150 g/5 oz) bought from a shop or supermarket.

dinner

mixed grill
2 low-fat or vegetarian sausages grilled with large mushrooms and tomatoes and served with 2 small oven-baked sweet potatoes. Accompany with a tomato salsa.

ALTERNATIVE

spaghetti bolognese
Made with 75 g (3 oz) lean beef mince or 125 g (4 oz) soya mince per portion with a jar of ready-made tomato sauce and extra mushrooms and onion added. Serve with 50 g (2 oz) spaghetti per person.

dessert

fresh pineapple slices

fit

It's been estimated by *Prima* magazine that our grandmothers burnt three times as many calories each day as we do, because they didn't use any labour-saving gadgets. So at least once a day aim to do a task by hand, instead of using an appliance to do it: easy examples include switching television channels over by hand instead of using the remote (don't laugh; after all, every 20 steps you take walking to the television and back burns a calorie) or washing dishes instead of using the dishwasher.

The ultimate workout, however, is washing the car yourself instead of taking it to the car wash – you'll burn roughly 200 calories in half an hour and give your arms a great workout.

feel good

Smile – it's been proved that your body can't tell the difference between a real smile and a fake one; simply the action of forcing your face into a grin causes mood-boosting endorphin chemicals to be released in the brain. If a low mood gets you down today (and potentially reaching for some sweet treats) stand in front of the mirror and just smile for a few minutes. Your mood will lift immediately.

fact

Many of us don't like berries such as raspberries because of the masses of tiny pips they contain. However, those pips have high levels of a vital natural chemical called ellagic acid. These have been shown to cause cancer cells to self-destruct.

day 3 **39**

berry breakfast

preparation: 15 minutes plus chilling | **serves:** 4

300 ml (½ pint) low-fat Greek yogurt

2 tablespoons clear honey

375 g (12 oz) raspberries

25 g (1 oz) porridge oats

1 Put the yogurt in a large bowl. Add the honey and fold in.

2 Divide one-third of the raspberries among 4 serving glasses. Cover with half the yogurt mixture. Scatter over some of the oats and more raspberries, dividing them among the glasses.

3 Repeat the layers, finishing with oats and a few raspberries. Chill in the refrigerator for 30 minutes before serving.

tip

This recipe is also great for a dessert. It can easily be varied using different fruits.

nutritional values per serving
Kcals **105 (445 kJ)**
Protein **1.8 g**
Carb **22.0 g**
Sodium **16 mg**
Fat **1.5 g**
Sat. fat **0.9 g**
GI **Low**

it's a wrap

preparation: 5 minutes | **cooking:** 8–10 minutes | **serves:** 4

1 teaspoon olive oil

2 garlic cloves, finely chopped

1 onion, finely chopped

250 g (8 oz) lean lamb stir-fry strips, cut small or halved

125 g (4 oz) mushrooms, finely chopped

1 small red pepper, cored, deseeded and sliced

2 tablespoons chopped fresh parsley

2 tablespoons chopped fresh mint

125 g (4 oz) cooked basmati rice

juice of 1 lemon

4 tablespoons low-fat Greek yogurt

2 tablespoons mint sauce

8 flour tortillas or flatbreads

¼ cucumber, cut into strips

rocket salad, to serve

1 To make the filling, heat the oil in a nonstick wok or pan and cook the garlic, onion and lamb strips for 3–4 minutes until brown. Add the mushrooms and pepper and cook for 2–3 minutes. Stir in the herbs, rice and lemon juice. Heat for a further 1–2 minutes.

2 Mix together the yogurt and mint sauce.

3 To assemble the wraps, place the flour tortillas on a clean work surface. Spread a dessertspoon of the yogurt mixture over each tortilla, top with a large spoonful of the filling and a few strips of cucumber.

4 Fold up to make a neat roll and serve immediately with a rocket salad.

nutritional values per serving
Kcals **408 (1723 kJ)**
Protein **25 g**
Carb **64.2 g**
Sodium **341 mg**
Fat **7.2 g**
Sat. fat **2.4 g**
GI **Low**

tip

Lean lamb is used here but other meat, such as pork, beef or chicken stir-fry strips, could be substituted. Try chickpeas for a vegetarian alternative.

day 4

By now you should be realizing how easy it is to fit low-GI eating into your daily life. Even if you're trying to combine losing weight with working in an office all day, these quick and easy meals make sticking to things ultra-simple. And almost all the lunches suggested here can easily be made in advance and taken to work from home.

food

breakfast

glass of unsweetened orange juice
150 ml (¼ pint)

grilled mushrooms on toast
Grill 2 large mushrooms and serve on 2 slices of toasted sourdough, soy/linseed or granary bread.

ALTERNATIVE
breakfast shake
Made by liquidizing together a banana, 150 ml (¼ pint) skimmed milk and 1 tablespoon oats.

snack

nectarine

lunch

chicken and chicory salad with sesame seed dressing
(see page 44)

ALTERNATIVE
can or carton of low-calorie vegetable soup
Serve with a large granary roll.

dessert

pot of low-fat yogurt with cherries
150 g (5 oz) natural yogurt, topped with a few cherries.

snack

large apple

dinner

oriental gingered salmon
(see page 45)

ALTERNATIVE
quinoa and roasted vegetables
Cook 75 g (3 oz) quinoa or bulgur wheat per person according to the directions on the packet. Roast aubergine, courgettes, red and green peppers in a spoonful of olive oil. Sprinkle with lemon juice and chopped herbs and serve on top of the quinoa or bulgur wheat.

dessert

raspberry blancmange
Make up 1 portion per person according to the instructions on the packet, using skimmed milk.

fact

Sunlight could make you slim. The action of sunlight on your skin produces vitamin D – and without this you absorb only 10 per of the calcium you take in (with it, this increases to 80–90 per cent). That is bad news for dieters, as recent research has revealed that calcium turns fat-storing cells into fat-burning ones! So aim to get outside for 30 minutes a day to boost your vitamin D levels.

fit

Many of us think running is only for the super-fit, but if you're already a regular walker, there's no reason you shouldn't start thinking about incorporating some light jogging into your daily workout (you'll burn twice as many calories per minute if you do).

The best way to get started is to alternate 30-second or one-minute bursts of jogging with four minutes of walking. If you're asked how hard you're working on a scale of ten, a sensible pace should feel like about seven or eight. As you get fitter, your jogging breaks can get longer and your walking breaks shorter. Next thing you know, you're a runner!

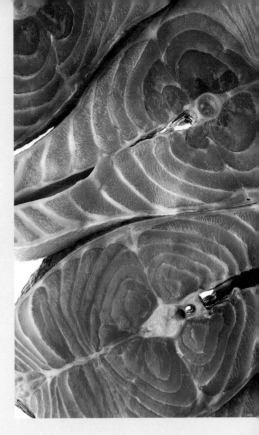

feel good

Doing something that absorbs your mind not only prevents you from snacking out of boredom but research is showing that it can boost your immune system and exercise your brain in a way that actually triggers it to create new cells (something that may help prevent age-related memory problems). Instead of slumping in front of the television each night, try to do something engaging tonight. If you're a creative type, get out some paints; if you're a fashionista, you may want to take up knitting; or just buy yourself a jigsaw and pick up those pieces. You'll be amazed how time will fly.

chicken and chicory salad with sesame seed dressing

preparation: 20 minutes | **serves:** 4

50 g (2 oz) lettuce, torn
into pieces

2 heads white chicory, sliced

¼ cucumber, diced

50 g (2 oz) broccoli florets,
cooked

2 large pink grapefruit, peeled
and segmented

125 g (4 oz) roast chicken, cut
into strips

400 g (13 oz) can chickpeas,
drained

1 large yellow pepper, cored,
deseeded and sliced

1 large green pepper, cored,
deseeded and sliced

250 g (8 oz) cherry tomatoes,
halved

4 slices grain and linseed bread

Dressing

½ teaspoon sugar

½ tablespoon Dijon mustard

2 tablespoons white wine vinegar

2 tablespoons olive oil

½ tablespoon sesame seeds

1 tablespoon soy sauce, optional

pepper

1 Toss the lettuce, chicory,
cucumber, broccoli and grapefruit
in a bowl.

2 Add the chicken, chickpeas,
peppers and tomatoes.

3 For the dressing mix the sugar,
mustard and vinegar and whisk.
Drizzle in the oil while still
whisking then add the pepper.

4 Dry-fry the sesame seeds until
lightly browned then toss with the
soy sauce, if liked, and quickly
cover with a lid. When cool, add
to the dressing.

5 Add the dressing to the salad
and serve the salad with slices
of grain and linseed bread.

nutritional values per serving
Kcals **188 (794 kJ)**
Protein **16.8 g**
Carb **23.8 g**
Sodium **167 mg**
Fat **4.0 g**
Sat. fat **0.7 g**
GI **Low**

tip

Chicory gives a wonderful
flavour but if you cannot
find it use cos lettuce or
pak choi. If you do not eat
chicken you could make this
recipe with tofu, nuts or
extra chickpeas.

oriental gingered salmon

preparation: 10 minutes | **cooking:** 6–10 minutes | **serves:** 4

½ **bunch spring onions, shredded**

2.5 cm (1 inch) **piece of fresh root ginger, peeled and cut into strips**

2 **tablespoons low-calorie American dry ginger ale or made-up low-calorie ginger cordial**

2 **tablespoons light soy sauce**

4 **salmon fillets, about** 125 g (4 oz) **each without skin**

cabbage, mangetout and 200 g (7 oz) **new potatoes, boiled in their skins, to serve**

1 Mix the spring onions, fresh ginger, ginger ale or cordial and soy sauce in a bowl.

2 Place the salmon in a covered frying pan and poach in the mixture for 3–5 minute each side. Top up with a little water if needed.

3 Serve with steamed cabbage, mangetout and new potatoes. Garnish with the spring onions and ginger and pour over a little of the ginger ale mixture.

nutritional values per serving
Kcals **233 (971 kJ)**
Protein **25.8 g**
Carb **1.3 g**
Sodium **57 mg**
Fat **13.8 g**
Sat. fat **2.4 g**
GI **Low**

day 5

You may not have realized it, but every day so far on this plan you've reached your recommended daily intake of five portions of fruit and vegetables. This was recently announced as one of the main healthy habits that lead to sustained weight loss, so it's great news for your diet – and vital for all-round well-being.

food

breakfast

bowl of soy and linseed cereal
Use 3 tablespoons cereal with 150 ml (¼ pint) skimmed milk. Top with a sliced small banana.

ALTERNATIVE
toast with peanut butter
Spread 1 teaspoon peanut butter on 2 slices of toasted sourdough, soy/linseed or granary bread.

snack

1 oat biscuit with a thin scraping of low-fat soft cheese

lunch

pasta with lentil and pepper sauce
(see page 48)

ALTERNATIVE
small tub of low-fat hummus and crudités
125 g (4 oz) hummus served with raw carrots, celery and cauliflower florets and 4 seeded rye crisp breads

dessert

2 kiwifruit

snack

low-fat natural fromage frais topped with blackberries
125 g (5 oz)

dinner

cos lettuce salad with Gorgonzola and walnuts
(see page 49)

Serve with oven-baked potato wedges made by slicing 1 large baking potato (175 g/6 oz) per person, into slender wedges, drizzling with some soy sauce and baking for approximately 20 minutes at the top of a hot oven, 200°C (400°F), Gas Mark 6, until crisp.

ALTERNATIVE
chicken salad
Made from a selection of salad leaves, coriander, sliced tomatoes and spring onions, up to 200 g (7 oz) drained canned chickpeas, 1 tablespoon pumpkin seeds and 125 g (4 oz) sliced grilled chicken breast tossed in 1 tablespoon low-calorie vinaigrette.

dessert

1 large pear

fact

Pears contain the vital mineral iodine, which helps to maximize thyroid function. As the thyroid is the gland that controls how many calories you burn each day, having it firing on all cylinders is vital for slimming success.

fit

Go swimming. Many of us only ever visit the pool during our summer break, but it's a great all-round body toner and perfect exercise for those who don't currently work out. Not only does swimming put no pressure on your joints, but your position in the water means that you actually feel less fatigued swimming than exercising in other ways at the same intensity.

If you're not a great swimmer, the pool isn't completely off the exercise schedule for you. Walking – or even running – in water over waist height creates extra resistance, boosting the toning effects of these exercises.

feel good

Take time over your meals today and every day: eating quickly is a common cause of bloating that adds to your waistline. Other belly-boosting activities include chewing gum, talking while eating and drinking from a sports-top bottle or while exercising – all of which trigger excess gas. If you do suffer, peppermint tea can help reduce the effects.

pasta with lentil and pepper sauce

preparation: 15 minutes | **cooking:** 35–40 minutes | **serves:** 4

125 g (4 oz) split red lentils

1 tablespoon olive oil

2 onions, chopped

2 small red peppers, cored, deseeded and chopped

4 large mushrooms, trimmed and sliced

1 garlic clove, crushed

2 tablespoons chopped fresh basil, plus extra to garnish

2 tablespoons chopped fresh oregano or parsley

400 g (13 oz) can tomatoes

2 tablespoons tomato purée

250 ml (8 fl oz) water

pinch of sugar

250 g (8 oz) wholewheat pasta

pepper

grated Parmesan cheese, to serve

1 Boil the lentils in water for 15 minutes. Drain.

2 Heat the oil in a nonstick pan and fry the onions and peppers for 10 minutes. Add the lentils, mushrooms, garlic, herbs, tomatoes, tomato purée, water, sugar and pepper.

3 Bring to the boil then turn down the heat and simmer gently, uncovered, for 15–20 minutes.

4 15 minutes before the sauce is ready half-fill a saucepan with water and bring to the boil. Add the pasta and boil rapidly for 10–12 minutes, or according to the instructions on the packet, until the pasta is cooked. Drain.

5 Garnish with fresh basil leaves and serve with grated Parmesan.

nutritional values per serving
Kcals **391 (1659 kJ)**
Protein **19.2 g**
Carb **71.4 g**
Sodium **162 mg**
Fat **5.3 g**
Sat. fat **0.7 g**
GI **Low**

cos lettuce salad with Gorgonzola and walnuts

preparation: 10 minutes | **serves:** 4

2 tablespoons olive oil

1 tablespoon good white wine vinegar

125 g (4 oz) Gorgonzola cheese

50 g (2 oz) shelled walnuts, coarsely chopped

1 cos lettuce, torn into bite-sized pieces

pepper

potato wedges, to serve

1 Put the oil, vinegar and a little pepper into a salad bowl and mix thoroughly. Add half the Gorgonzola and mash it well with a fork.

2 Add half the chopped walnuts and all the lettuce, and toss until evenly coated with the dressing.

3 Top with the remaining Gorgonzola, cut into small pieces, and the rest of the chopped walnuts.

nutritional values per serving
Kcals **250 (1050 kJ)**
Protein **9 g**
Carb **1 g**
Sodium **346 mg**
Fat **23 g**
Sat. fat **8 g**
GI **Low**

tip

This really light recipe will serve 8 as a dinner-party starter. You can vary the ingredients by using Roquefort instead of Gorgonzola if you prefer a stronger taste.

day 6

If you started this diet on a Monday, it is now the weekend with all the temptations that can occur. However, by kicking off with a hearty breakfast – and finishing the day with a meal that definitely won't make you feel as if you're dieting – you're assured of success.

food

breakfast

kedgeree
(see page 52)

ALTERNATIVE
glass of tropical fruit juice
150 ml (¼ pint)

pot of low-fat yogurt and raspberries, plus 1 crumpet or pikelet, toasted

snack

mix of seeds and nuts
25 g (1 oz)

lunch

grilled tomatoes
Serve on 2 slices of toasted sourdough, soy/linseed or granary bread.

ALTERNATIVE
can or carton of low-fat lentil soup
Serve with a granary roll.

dessert

2 large plums

snack

1 oat biscuit topped with apple slices

dinner

grilled sirloin steak with 25 g (1 oz) couscous, salad leaves and three-bean salad
(see page 53)
Grill a 125 g (4 oz) steak. Make up 75 g (3 oz) couscous according to the instructions on the packet and serve with the bean salad and a selection of salad leaves.

ALTERNATIVE
grilled veggie burger
Fill 2 small pitta breads with strips of a grilled vegetable burger, grated carrot, couscous made according to the instructions on the packet, chopped tomato and strips of cucumber with chopped mint and a low-fat yogurt dressing.

dessert

baked banana and low-fat fromage frais

Use 1 banana and ½ pot (75 g/ 3 oz) low-fat natural fromage frais. Serve sprinkled with a few chocolate strands.

fit

Skipping is an incredible calorie-burning exercise, using up more than 600 calories an hour, which is equivalent to running at 10 kph (6 mph). The best thing about it, however, is that it can easily be done in the privacy of your own home – all you need is a skipping rope and some supportive trainers to prevent ankle injuries.

Aim for five minutes today (you may need to do it in one-minute bursts), then build up to 15–20 minutes a day.

feel good

While it's meant to be a break from the working week, the weekend is spent by many of us rushing around even more intensely than usual. If you've got a hectic day ahead, at least spend five minutes relaxing.

A quick meditation technique is to lie down or sit in a chair and gradually relax each part of your body, feeling it grow looser and heavier. Become aware of your breathing and gradually slow it down, so that you carefully decelerate your exhaled breath until it is slower than your inhaled breath. As thoughts enter your head, see them roll up and out of your mind – rather like watching the credits at the end of a film. After five (or more) minutes, gradually stop the relaxation by gently clenching and then relaxing each muscle of your body, starting from your jaw and moving down to your feet. Now open your eyes and see how refreshed you feel.

fact

The beans that you find in today's three-bean salad are a great source of soluble fibre, which has a beneficial effect in helping to lower blood-cholesterol levels and blood-sugar levels. Other good sources of soluble fibre include oats, peas and lentils.

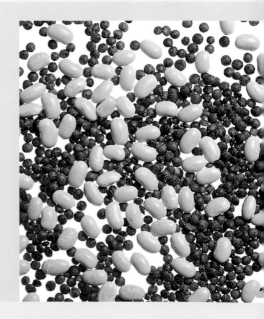

kedgeree

preparation: 10 minutes | **cooking:** 20 minutes | **serves:** 4

250 g (8 oz) smoked haddock

300 ml (½ pint) low-fat coconut milk

125 g (4 oz) brown lentils

1 teaspoon vegetable oil

1 small onion, chopped finely

125 g (4 oz) button mushrooms, trimmed and sliced

1 teaspoon tandoori paste

175 g (6 oz) cooked brown basmati rice

2 hard-boiled eggs, chopped

pepper

coriander, to garnish

1 Poach the haddock in the coconut milk for 8 minutes and allow to cool. Reserve the milk. Remove the skin from the cooled haddock and flake the flesh.

2 Meanwhile, cook the lentils in boiling water for 15 minutes and drain.

3 Heat the oil and cook the onion for 2 minutes, add the sliced mushrooms and cook for a further 2 minutes. Add the tandoori paste.

4 Add the rice and lentils to the onion and mushrooms. Add enough of the reserved coconut milk to moisten the mixture and season with pepper. Mix well then add the haddock and eggs.

5 Serve immediately, garnished with a sprig of coriander.

nutritional values per serving
Kcals **436 (1830 kJ)**
Protein **27.4 g**
Carb **54.5 g**
Sodium **592 mg**
Fat **12.3 g**
Sat. fat **1.0 g**
GI **Low**

three-bean salad

preparation: 10 minutes | **cooking:** 5 minutes | **serves:** 4

tip

There are endless variations for this easy salad. You can substitute a small can of sweetcorn for one of the cans of beans; add other salad vegetables, such as cherry tomatoes, radish slices, cucumber and grated carrots; or add cooked chicken or flaked tuna. Mix the salad with cooked rice or pasta for a meal on its own.

nutritional values per serving
Kcals **212 (898 kJ)**
Protein **14.4 g**
Carb **34.8 g**
Sodium **476 mg**
Fat **2.6 g**
Sat. fat **0.4 g**
GI **Low**

125 g (4 oz) sliced green beans

400 g (13 oz) can red kidney beans, rinsed and drained

400 g (13 oz) can black-eyed beans, rinsed and drained

400 g (13 oz) can chickpeas, rinsed and drained

1 small red onion, finely chopped

1 tablespoon balsamic vinegar

1 tablespoon lemon juice

1 Cook the green beans in boiling water for 5 minutes. Drain and then cool by rinsing under a cold tap.

2 Mix the green beans, kidney beans, black-eyed beans, chickpeas and onion together.

3 Pour over the vinegar and lemon juice and toss to coat evenly. Serve.

day 7

At the end of today you'll be halfway through your diet, and hopefully you've now realized how easy losing weight the GI way can be. If you are having trouble motivating yourself, however, spend a few minutes at the end of the day thinking about all the positive feelings you have experienced this week to encourage you to stick with things next week, too.

food

breakfast

glass of cranberry juice
150 ml (¼ pint)

bowl of porridge
Use 3 tablespoons porridge and make it up with water according to the instruction on the packet. Serve with 200 ml (7 fl oz) skimmed milk.

ALTERNATIVE
toasted bread with pumpkin seeds and peanut butter, plus two apricots or plums
If you have a bread-maker or make your own bread by hand try adding pumpkin seeds to the mix; if using ready-made bread, toast 2 slices and spread with peanut butter then sprinkle with pumpkin seeds.

snack

slice of melon

lunch

cheesy potato bake
(see page 56)

ALTERNATIVE
roast chicken breast

Serve 125 g (4 oz) chicken breast with a mixture of 175 g (6 oz) small new potatoes in their skins, chunks of sweet potatoes and butternut squash roasted in 1 teaspoon rapeseed oil, together with boiled carrots and peas. Make gravy with chicken gravy mix and the water in which the vegetables were boiled.

dessert

prune and apricot pudding
(see page 57)

snack

dried berry mix
25 g (1 oz)

dinner

spicy prawns, basmati and ready stir-fried vegetables

Boil basmati rice according to the instruction on the packet, allowing 50 g (2 oz) per person, and prepare the stir-fried vegetables as directed. Toss 75 g (3 oz) cooked prawns, or 150 g (5 oz) tofu, in 1 teaspoon sweet chilli sauce. Pile the rice on to a plate, top with the stir-fried vegetables and prawns.

ALTERNATIVE
open sandwich

Made with 1 slice of sourdough, soy/linseed or granary bread spread with a thin layer of yeast extract or beef extract and topped with 100 g (3½ oz) cottage cheese, sliced cucumber, tomatoes and strips of yellow pepper.

dessert

2 handfuls fresh cherries
Serve with 2 tablespoons silken tofu or low-fat fromage frais.

feel good

Spend five minutes today thinking about what you've learnt about healthy eating so far on the plan – maybe you're surprised at how small a portion of pasta should be or just how easy it is to eat five portions of fruit and vegetables a day. This 'learning' approach to dieting has recently been identified by Yale University researchers as one of the most important factors not only in losing weight – but also in keeping it off.

fit

Make the most of extra time at the weekend and move your workout outside, by taking a hike in the countryside (or at least the local park). Take a friend, your partner, the children or the dog, and walk briskly for at least an hour. Ideally, you should be walking fast enough to feel a little out of breath, but still able to carry on a conversation – this not only helps pass the time, but also indicates that you're in the maximum fat-burning zone for your body. If you cannot talk and walk at the same time, slow down a little.

fact

Purple fruits are packed with antioxidants, so it's no surprise that prunes, in which all those vital nutrients are condensed during the drying process, have been found to contain the highest level of antioxidants of any fruit.

cheesy potato bake

preparation: 15 minutes | **cooking:** 30 minutes | **serves:** 4

15 g (½ oz) butter

1 kg (2 lb) potatoes, skins left on, sliced

1 cauliflower, broken into florets

420 g (14 oz) can butter beans, drained

600 ml (1 pint) skimmed milk

cornflour or thickening granules

2 teaspoons Dijon mustard

garlic clove, cut in half

large pinch of grated nutmeg

125 g (4 oz) low-fat Cheddar cheese, grated

pepper

1 Lightly grease a shallow baking dish with the butter.

2 Boil the potatoes and cauliflower together and simmer gently for 10 minutes or until tender. Add the butter beans to the mixture and simmer for 1 minute. Drain.

3 Make a white sauce with the skimmed milk and cornflour and stir in the mustard.

4 Rub the cut sides of the garlic over the inside of the greased baking dish. Put the potatoes, cauliflower and beans into the dish and pour the white sauce over the top. Sprinkle over the grated nutmeg and pepper.

5 Sprinkle grated cheese over the top of the potatoes. Place under a hot preheated grill for 5 minutes or until the cheese has melted and the top is crispy and golden brown.

nutritional values per serving
Kcals **460 (1944 kJ)**
Protein **28.0 g**
Carb **69.3 g**
Sodium **1062 mg**
Fat **9.9 g**
Sat. fat **4.4 g**
GI **Low**

prune and apricot pudding

preparation: 10 minutes | **cooking:** 30–40 minutes | **serves:** 4

50 g (2 oz) low-fat spread

50 g (2 oz) soft brown sugar

1 egg, beaten

50 g (2 oz) self-raising wholemeal flour

1 tablespoon skimmed milk

50 g (2 oz) ready-to-eat prunes

50 g (2 oz) ready-to-eat dried apricots

custard made with skimmed milk, to serve

nutritional values per serving
Kcals **197 (829 kJ)**
Protein **4.7 g**
Carb **31.3 g**
Sodium **157 mg**
Fat **6.9 g**
Sat. fat **1.9 g**
GI **Low**

1 Beat together the low-fat spread and sugar until light and fluffy, then add the egg, a little at a time, making sure the egg is well absorbed on each addition. (You can add a little flour with the egg if you wish.) Fold in the remaining flour and add the milk to the mix. It should have a soft dropping consistency.

2 Lightly grease an 18 cm (7 inch) ovenproof dish. Put in a little water and arrange the prunes and apricots over the base.

3 Pour over the pudding mix and spread evenly. Bake in a preheated oven, 180°C (350°F), Gas Mark 4, for 30–40 minutes.

4 Serve warm with custard.

day 8

It's the first day of a new week, so when you wake up this morning spend a few minutes repeating to yourself a positive statement, such as 'I can stick to this plan again this week' or 'I am going to make healthy choices today'. This switches on the goal-orientated part of your brain and actively helps you focus on your aims more easily.

food

breakfast

glass of orange juice
150 ml (¼ pint)

wholegrain bagel with low-fat soft cheese
Spread the low-fat soft or cottage cheese thinly on 1 wholegrain bagel.

ALTERNATIVE
bowl of grain or bran cereal
3 tablespoons cereal with 200 ml (7 fl oz) skimmed milk.

snack

handful of gooseberries or greengages, in season, or 1 pear

lunch

toasted peanut and wild rice salad
(see page 60)

ALTERNATIVE
spicy sausage and pasta salad
(see page 61)

dessert

frozen yogurt
150 g (5 oz)

snack

pumpkin seeds
25 g (1 oz)

dinner

trout with vegetables

Cook 125 g (4 oz) trout fillet according to the instructions on the pack and serve with steamed mangetout and broccoli and 50 g (2 oz) boiled potatoes mashed with ½ well-cooked parsnip and 4 tablespoons chickpeas.

ALTERNATIVE
spicy vegetable burger

Grill 125 g (4 oz) spicy vegetable burger and serve with 50 g (2 oz) boiled potatoes mashed with ½ well-cooked parsnip and 4 tablespoons chickpeas, plus mushy peas made from a pack of quick-cooked dried peas and gravy.

dessert

cream jelly

Make sugar-free jelly according to the packet instructions but use all or a proportion of skimmed milk instead of water.

fact

Seasonal fruit such as greengages is a great way to liven up your diet. It may also discourage overeating. According to the American Dietetic Association, we don't tend to overeat unfamiliar foods, so experimenting could actually make you thinner.

fit

Every day this week choose one place that you would normally drive to (or take public transport to) and do the same errand on foot, on bike or even on skates, if you're that way inclined. It might be driving to pick up the morning paper, getting the bus to the station, nipping to get that pint of milk you've forgotten, or heading to a doctor's appointment at lunchtime.

In future you could even make it a rule for yourself that any journey that would take less than five minutes by car or bus will now be carried out by 'alternative' transport.

feel good

By now people may have started to notice that you're eating differently – but don't be tempted to tell everyone that you're trying to lose weight. Sometimes it's better to tell people that you're trying to eat more nutritionally for the sake of your health, rather than for your waistline. This prevents them from trying to tempt you with chocolate or sweets.

toasted peanut and wild rice salad

preparation: 5 minutes | **cooking:** 30 minutes | **serves:** 4

125 g (4 oz) basmati rice

25 g (1 oz) wild rice

1 bunch of spring onions, chopped

125 g (4 oz) sultanas

125 g (4 oz) toasted peanuts

4 tablespoons balsamic vinegar

1 tablespoon sunflower oil

green salad leaves, to serve

nutritional values per serving
Kcals **427 (1786 kJ)**
Protein **12.0 g**
Carb **56.0 g**
Sodium **8 mg**
Fat **17.5 g**
Sat. fat **3.1 g**
GI **Low**

1 Cook both types of rice according to the instruction on the packet then rinse in cold water.

2 Mix the cooked rice, spring onions, sultanas and peanuts in a large bowl.

3 Pour the vinegar and oil into a small bowl and whisk, then stir into the salad.

4 Serve with green salad leaves.

tip

This easy-to-make salad is convenient for picnics and packed lunches and is another useful storecupboard recipe. Try adding cucumber, lettuce and tomatoes too.

spicy sausage and pasta salad

preparation: 10 minutes | **cooking:** 15 minutes | **serves:** 4

tip

This is another easy-to-make salad that's suitable for picnics and packed lunches. The sausages are low in GI – so try different flavours. Vegetarian sausages can also be used, or cooked chicken or hot steak cut into small pieces could be substituted for the sausages.

250 g (8 oz) wholewheat pasta spirals

8 low-fat sausages, about 450 g (14 ½ oz)

1 bunch of spring onions

½ head of celery

50 ml (2 fl oz) low-fat honey and mustard salad dressing

cos lettuce, to serve

1 Cook the pasta according to the instruction on the packet and then rinse in cold water.

2 Prick and then grill the sausages, turning them constantly to reduce the fat content. Drain off the fat and leave the sausages to cool.

3 When cooled, slice the sausages into thick chunks. Cut the spring onions and celery into chunks.

4 Mix the pasta, sausages, celery and spring onions with the salad dressing.

5 Serve with cos lettuce leaves.

nutritional values per serving
Kcals **418 (1763 kJ)**
Protein **23.9 g**
Carb **52.8 g**
Sodium **1074 mg**
Fat **13.9 g**
Sat. fat **4.5 g**
GI **Low**

day 9

You may find that you're getting compliments from other people telling you how well you're looking. This is partly because you have started to lose weight by now, but also because all that water you're drinking – and the high levels of fruit and vegetables, combined with low levels of sugar – means that your skin will have developed a healthy glow.

food

breakfast

half a grapefruit

baked beans on sourdough toast
4 tablespoons baked beans on 1 slice of toasted sourdough and flax seed bread.

ALTERNATIVE
granary toast with banana
2 slices of toasted granary bread topped with a sliced banana.

snack

4 Brazil nuts

lunch

ready-made chicken salad
Accompany a bought ready-made chicken salad (with low-calorie

dressing) with 4 rye multigrain and sunflower seed crisp breads.

ALTERNATIVE

ham and salad sandwich
Made from 2 slices of soy/linseed bread, lettuce, tomato and 25 g (1 oz) lean ham.

dessert

summer pudding
(see page 65)

snack

large nectarine or peach

dinner

cauliflower and chickpea curry
(see page 64)

ALTERNATIVE

salmon fishcakes and spicy chips
Use 50 g (2 oz) canned salmon per person, mixed with cooked lentils and mashed potatoes and bound together with a beaten egg and rolled in breadcrumbs before frying in 1 tablespoon oil. Serve with spicy chips made by sprinkling chip-shaped pieces of sweet potato with soy or chilli sauce and oven baking them for about 20 minutes, together with a large green salad.

dessert

melon and raspberries
Cut a slice of melon and serve with raspberries.

fit

Circuit training is a great way to burn calories without getting bored. Build up to being able to repeat the following five exercises four times. You should be working at a rate at which you can speak but not hold a conversation.

1 **March on the spot** for one minute.

2 **Walking lunges:** take a large step forward, then lower your hips in a dip. Hold for a second, lift up and take another step.

Repeat, moving back and forth across the room for one minute.

3 **Star jumps:** standing with your legs hip-width apart, jump up and land with your legs closed; repeat and land with your legs open. Repeat for one minute.

4 **Place a ball** (or similar small item) on the floor and jump over it from side to side. Repeat for one minute.

5 **Walk up and down the stairs** for one minute.

feel good

By now sugar cravings should be a thing of the past for you – your blood-sugar levels should be completely under control, although you might find that you still crave sugary treats out of habit at around 3 p.m. If you do, spend a few seconds sitting still, and visualize a rainbow or some roses in your mind. New research from Flinders University in Australia has discovered that this helps stop food cravings in their tracks. This is probably because it takes your mind off them and replaces them with something pleasant, which your mind enjoys thinking about.

fact

Brazil nuts contain high levels of selenium, which acts as an antioxidant and helps the body fight infections and coronary heart disease.

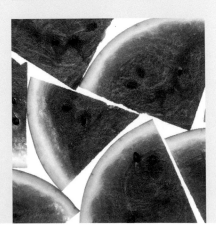

cauliflower and chickpea curry

preparation: 10 minutes | **cooking:** 30 minutes | **serves:** 4

1 tablespoon rapeseed oil

1 large onion, chopped

1–2 garlic cloves, crushed

2 tablespoons medium curry paste

1 cauliflower, cooked and broken into florets

400 g (13 oz) can chickpeas, drained

2 large potatoes with skins, diced

400 g (13 oz) can chopped tomatoes

handful of coriander leaves

basmati rice, to serve

1 Heat the oil in a nonstick pan. Fry the onion and garlic until soft.

2 Add the curry paste and cook for 1 minute.

3 Add the cauliflower, chickpeas, diced potatoes and tomatoes. Bring to the boil, cover and simmer for 20–30 minutes until the potatoes are cooked.

4 Remove the lid and boil a few minutes more until the liquid is reduced and thickened. Add the coriander leaves.

5 Serve with basmati rice.

tip

This is an easy and economical curry to make. If you like your curries really hot add some chilli powder. Other vegetables, such as courgettes and mushrooms, can be used in addition to the cauliflower and chickpeas. If you prefer, 100 g (4 oz) diced cooked lamb or beef can also be added.

nutritional values per serving
Kcals **285 (1201 kJ)**
Protein **13.9 g**
Carb **41.3 g**
Sodium **345 mg**
Fat **8.3 g**
Sat. fat **0.6 g**
GI **Low**

summer pudding

preparation: 30 minutes plus chilling | **cooking:** 10 minutes | **serves:** 4

500 g (1 lb) mixture of plums, redcurrants, apples and raspberries

25 g (1 oz) caster sugar

75 ml (3 fl oz) water

6 slices of day-old grain bread

low-fat natural fromage frais, to serve

tip

Look out for bargains in late summer when fruit such as plums and damsons are in season and freeze them ready for use in the winter.

nutritional values per serving
Kcals **164 (699 kJ)**
Protein **5.2 g**
Carb **35.2 g**
Sodium **223 mg**
Fat **1.5 g**
Sat. fat **0.2 g**
GI **Low**

1 Put the fruit in a pan with the sugar and the water. Gently heat to a simmer and cook for 10 minutes. Strain the fruit, catching the juice in a bowl.

2 Cut out 2 circles of bread to fit the top and bottom of a 750 ml (1¼ pint) pudding basin. Shape the rest to fit the sides. Dip the slices in the reserved fruit juice and line the basin.

3 Spoon the fruit into the basin and put the final circle of bread on top. Cover with a saucer and place some cans or weights on top. Chill overnight.

4 Remove the weights and saucer and invert a plate on top. Holding tightly in place, turn the basin over to release the pudding.

5 Serve with low-fat fromage frais.

day 10

You're nearing the end of the official two-week plan, and if your willpower is going to fail you, it will be around now, so this morning spend a few minutes looking at yourself in the mirror. Notice any changes, but more importantly focus on any areas of your body that you really like. It's believed this doubles the chance that you'll see a diet out to its end without problems.

food

ALTERNATIVE
smoked mackerel with black pepper
125 g (4 oz) peppered smoked mackerel with a large green salad and a granary roll.

dessert

bowl of strawberries with low-fat natural fromage frais

breakfast

potato cakes
(see page 68)

ALTERNATIVE
bowl of sugar-free muesli
2 tablespoons sugar-free muesli with 200 ml (7 fl oz) skimmed milk and topped with grated apple.

snack

2 plums

lunch

egg sandwich
Made from 2 slices of granary bread filled with a sliced hard-boiled egg, watercress and 1 teaspoon of light mayonnaise.

snack

low-fat chocolate mousse
Small tub (150 g/5 oz) bought from a shop or supermarket.

dinner

spicy beef
(see page 69)

ALTERNATIVE

cauliflower cheese
Use a quarter of a whole cauliflower and a cheese sauce made with 25 g (1 oz) low-fat cheese and 150 ml (¼ pint) skimmed milk thickened with cornflour. Serve with 200 g (7 oz) baked beans.

dessert

pineapple and raspberries
2 slices of pineapple canned in its own juice and a handful of raspberries.

fit

Bouncing on a rebounder (a mini-trampoline) isn't just a fun way to burn around 400 calories an hour; it's also believed to be one of the primary ways in which you can increase the activity of the lymph system, which carries waste products out of your body. A stagnant lymph system is one of the contributory causes of cellulite, so if you suffer from this, rebounding may be good exercise to try (weight training is also incredibly effective at fighting cellulite). You'll find rebounders in most sports stores.

feel good

Aim for *lagom* in your life. This Swedish word means 'just enough' and harks back to an old Viking tradition whereby people used to bond over a communal cup of mead; they didn't want to take too much or there wouldn't be enough for everyone else. And that's a good way to think about the rest of your life: too much work doesn't leave enough time for family and friends; too many family chores don't leave enough time for you. Think *lagom* in everything you do – including weight loss; in fact, you'll notice that today you get a chocolaty treat to help you do just that.

fact

Beef is an excellent source of iron, which many people (especially women) lack. That's a pity, because low iron levels lead to fatigue – and to a sluggish metabolic rate.

potato cakes

preparation: 10 minutes | **cooking:** 6 minutes | **serves:** 4

250 g (8 oz) mashed potato

198 g (7 oz) can sweetcorn, drained

2 tablespoons oatbran

1 small egg, lightly beaten

1 tablespoon vegetable oil

tomatoes and mushrooms, to serve

1 Mix the mashed potato, sweetcorn, oatbran and egg in a large bowl. Then divide the mixture into 4 and pat it into flat rounds.

2 Heat the oil in a large nonstick pan and add the cakes one at a time. Cook for 3 minutes then flip over and cook for a further 3 minutes.

3 Serve with tomatoes and mushrooms.

tip

Potato cakes make a substantial breakfast. They can also be served at other meals and are very good with baked beans.

nutritional values per serving
Kcals **148 (621 kJ)**
Protein **4.5 g**
Carb **21.5 g**
Sodium **26 mg**
Fat **5.4 g**
Sat. fat **0.8 g**
GI **Low**

spicy beef

preparation: 10 minutes | **cooking:** 15 minutes | **serves:** 4

1 teaspoon olive oil

1 onion, sliced

1–2 garlic cloves, crushed

2.5 cm (1 inch) piece of root ginger, peeled and finely chopped

25 g (1 oz) plain flour

½ teaspoon turmeric

½ teaspoon chilli powder

400 g (13 oz) beef, cut into strips

1 tablespoon soy sauce

25 g (1 oz) dry-roasted peanuts

500 ml (17 fl oz) skimmed milk

stir-fried vegetables, to serve

1 Heat the oil in a pan and fry the onion, garlic and ginger for 3–5 minutes. Mix the flour and spices in a bowl and coat the beef, shaking off excess and reserving the rest of the mix.

2 Add the beef to the pan and fry for 3 minutes or until browned.

3 Stir in the reserved flour mix, soy sauce and peanuts. Cook while stirring for another 2 minutes.

4 Slowly add the milk and stir until the sauce thickens and boils. Cook for 1 minute then cover and simmer for 5 minutes.

5 Serve with stir-fried vegetables.

nutritional values per serving
Kcals **257 (1078 kJ)**
Protein **27.4 g**
Carb **14.2 g**
Sodium **215 mg**
Fat **10.7 g**
Sat. fat **2.6 g**
GI **Low**

tip

Beef is a great source of iron. A surprising way to change this dish is to use liver instead of the beef, or try it with pork. The sauce is delicious and really easy to make – the secret is to add the milk slowly. If you want another variation, try using low-fat coconut milk.

day 11

Yesterday's chocolate treat should have encouraged you a little, but another great trick to try today is to put on a pair of trousers (or other item of clothing) that normally feels a little snug. By now it should feel nicely comfortable – if not a bit loose. You should also be noticing that your daily 'fit' task is becoming much easier as your fitness level starts to build.

food
breakfast

breakfast smoothie
Made by liquidizing together a handful of berries and 150 ml (¼ pint) skimmed milk.

ALTERNATIVE
cranberry granola
(see page 72)
Serve with 200 ml (7 fl oz) skimmed milk.

snack

2 oat biscuits topped with a very thin slice of low-fat cheese

lunch

falafels

4–5 falafels made according to the instructions on the packet and served in a small wholemeal pitta with shredded lettuce, cucumber and carrots and low-fat natural yogurt flavoured with fresh mint.

ALTERNATIVE
tuna salad

50 g (2 oz) canned tuna, drained, and served with a large helping of green salad, cherry tomatoes, 1 teaspoon low-calorie Italian salad dressing and 4 seeded crisp breads.

dessert

slices of mango and cherries

snack

pear

dinner

turkey burgers
(see page 73)
Serve with granary rolls, tomato and red onion relish, and crisp salad leaves or roasted vegetables, such as peppers, mushrooms, aubergine, courgettes and tomatoes.

ALTERNATIVE
vegetable stir-fry

Made from vegetables of your choice, served on 50 g (2 oz) dried egg noodles. Add 1 teaspoon sweet chilli sauce to taste.

dessert

instant whipped pudding

Make 1 portion from a packet, using skimmed milk.

fit

Take some time to stretch. Lengthening the muscles not only helps release tension in the body, but also helps improve posture (and good posture makes you look actively 3 kg/6½ lb thinner).

A great morning and night stretch for your shoulders, legs and upper body is to stand in a doorway with one arm resting on the door frame. Take a step forward and dip into as low a lunge as possible. Hold for 30–60 seconds, then repeat using the other arm.

feel good

Fluid retention is a common problem for many women – and adds extra weight on the scales and extra size to your waistline. To find out if you suffer from this, press your forefinger on your leg in three or four different places. If it stays white for more than a few seconds after you lift the finger away, you're carrying extra fluid.

Drinking 2 litres (3½ pints) of water every day will help with this, but for an extra boost, add two cups of dandelion tea to your daily diet from now until the end of the plan. This is a natural diuretic, but unlike other diuretic drinks, it doesn't negatively interfere with your vitamin and mineral levels.

fact

GI eating really is suitable for the whole family – in fact, children who follow a low-GI diet tend to have less of a problem with obesity than other children. So your entire family can follow this plan, if you adjust the portion sizes to suit their appetites and activity levels.

cranberry granola

preparation: 10 minutes | **cooking:** 4–6 hours | **serves:** 4

175 g (6 oz) rolled oats

50 g (2 oz) dried cranberries

1 tablespoon sunflower oil

2 tablespoons honey

skimmed milk or low-fat natural yogurt, to serve

1 Place all the ingredients in a warm mixing bowl and stir until the oats are covered evenly with the oil and honey.

2 Turn out on to a nonstick baking plate, making sure that there are no lumps.

3 Place in the bottom of a warm oven, 100°C (200°F), less than Gas Mark 1, for about 4–6 hours, stirring occasionally to prevent sticking or browning.

4 When crispy remove and allow to cool. Store in an airtight container. The mixture will keep fresh for several days if kept free of moisture.

5 Serve with skimmed milk or low-fat yogurt.

tip

Granola is very easy to make. You may also like to mix in a little ground cinnamon or ginger before baking.

nutritional values per serving
Kcals **124 (523 kJ)**
Protein **2.8 g**
Carb **22.1 g**
Sodium **8 mg**
Fat **3.3 g**
Sat. fat **0.2 g**
GI **Low**

turkey burgers

preparation: 16 minutes plus chilling | **cooking:** 12–14 minutes | **serves:** 4

250 g (8 oz) extra lean minced turkey

1 small onion, grated

2 small courgettes, grated

1 teaspoon soy sauce

1 egg

50 g (2 oz) breadcrumbs

50 g (2 oz) oatmeal

pepper

4 granary rolls, tomato and red onion relish, and crisp salad leaves or vegetables, to serve

nutritional values per serving
Kcals **258 (1087 kJ)**
Protein **33.5 g**
Carb **20.7 g**
Sodium **214 mg**
Fat **5.1 g**
Sat. fat **1.1 g**
GI **Low**

1 Mix all the ingredients together in a bowl. Cover and leave in the refrigerator for 30 minutes. Divide the mixture into 4 and shape the burgers with your hands.

2 Preheat the grill to medium. Line a grill rack with foil and arrange the burgers on it. Cook for 6–7 minutes each side until thoroughly cooked.

3 Serve with granary rolls, tomato and red onion relish and crisp salad leaves or a selection of roasted vegetables, such as peppers, mushrooms, aubergines, courgettes and tomatoes.

day 12

Only three days to go now, so stay focused. Many people start to slip up towards the end of a diet plan, as their attention wanders and they start nibbling things from the refrigerator or using their eyes rather than their scales to determine portion sizes. Don't let this happen to you – remember, calories still count, even if you are eating low-GI foods.

food

breakfast

glass of red grapefruit juice
150 ml (¼ pint)

bowl of bran cereal or low-sugar muesli
3 tablespoons cereal with 200 ml (7 fl oz) skimmed milk.

ALTERNATIVE
egg bagel
½ bagel topped with 1 egg, poached or scrambled with a little skimmed milk.

snack

2 oat biscuits spread with 1 teaspoon each of cottage cheese

lunch

pork and pineapple fajitas
(see page 77)

ALTERNATIVE
baked potato with tuna and sweetcorn
250 g (8 oz) potato topped with 50 g (2 oz) canned tuna and sweetcorn.

dessert

slice of melon

snack

packet of nuts, seeds and raisins
25 g (1 oz)

dinner

oriental noodles
(see page 76)

ALTERNATIVE
Soup followed by ham salad
1 200 g (7 oz) can of tomato or vegetable soup
1 slice of lean ham (25 g/1 oz) with sliced tomatoes, cucumber, grated carrots, spring onions, peppers and Little Gem lettuce. Serve with 4 large seeded rye crisp breads.

dessert

apricots with low-fat natural yogurt
Use either fresh apricots or canned apricots in their own juice.

fit

Try some 'interval training'. This fitness-boosting activity can be incorporated into whatever exercise you enjoy doing – be it cycling, walking, swimming or jogging. To carry it out, every two to four minutes (depending on your fitness level) add a 30-second spurt, during which you work as hard as you can. Recover, then repeat. Do three or four of these spurts during your workout to strengthen your lungs and maximize the metabolic boost that the exercise gives you.

feel good

It's the end of the week and so, even with the potent fatigue-fighting powers of the GI plan, you could be feeling a little tired today. Revive yourself with a simple energizing acupressure technique. All you need to do is locate the little dips that appear around the hairline on the back of your neck, and about two finger widths on either side of your spine. Rest the fingers of each hand on the back of your head and use your thumbs to gently put pressure on this energizing point for 30 seconds.

fact

Even if you don't keep up all your low-GI habits when the 14-day diet plan is over, simply adding a low-GI mid-morning snack to your day will help you feel more energized than normal.

oriental noodles

preparation: 20 minutes | **cooking:** 15 minutes | **serves:** 4

125 ml (4 fl oz) light soy sauce

2 tablespoons dry rice wine vinegar

2 tablespoons plum sauce

500 g (1 lb) lean pork fillet, cut into strips

250 g (8 oz) dried medium egg noodles

4 small carrots

1 red pepper, cored and seeded

125 g (4 oz) mangetout

175 g (6 oz) baby sweetcorn

3 tablespoons sunflower oil

4 spring onions, sliced

pepper

1 Mix together the soy sauce, vinegar, plum sauce and some pepper in a shallow dish. Add the pork and coat well. Let stand for 30 minutes in a covered dish in the refrigerator.

2 Cook the noodles in boiling water for 5 minutes, then drain.

3 Cut the carrots into 5 cm (2 inch) batons. Slice the red pepper into 5 cm (2 inch) strips. Blanch all the vegetables except the spring onions for 2 minutes in boiling water and drain.

4 Heat the oil in a nonstick wok or pan. Stir-fry the pork until just browned. Add the blanched vegetables and cook quickly. Add the noodles and marinade. Stir-fry for 5 minutes.

5 Sprinkle with the spring onions to serve.

tip

This is an easy recipe to make and it includes a good selection of vegetables. You can vary the vegetables and use courgettes, red kidney beans, frozen peas and bean sprouts if you want. Nowadays you can buy pre-cooked noodles, which cuts down on the cooking time.

nutritional values per serving
Kcals **316 (1327 kJ)**
Protein **32.4 g**
Carb **15.1 g**
Sodium **591 mg**
Fat **13.9 g**
Sat. fat **2.8 g**
GI **Low**

pork and pineapple fajitas

preparation: 10 minutes | **cooking:** 10 minutes | **serves:** 4

½ tablespoon olive oil

1 small onion, chopped

200 g (7 oz) lean pork mince

2 garlic cloves, crushed

1 red pepper, cored, deseeded and chopped

4 large mushrooms, sliced

2 canned pineapple rings, chopped

2 tablespoons pineapple juice

1 tablespoon tomato sauce

1 tablespoon soy sauce

pinch of chilli powder

125 g (4 oz) bean sprouts

8 tortilla wraps

salad leaves, to serve

nutritional values per serving
Kcals **334 (1412 kJ)**
Protein **18.6 g**
Carb **56.7 g**
Sodium **419 g**
Fat **5.2 g**
Sat. fat **1.2 g**
GI **Low**

1 Heat the oil in a nonstick pan and fry the onion until soft.

2 Add the pork and the garlic to the pan and fry for 3–4 minutes until cooked.

3 Add all the other ingredients except for the bean sprouts and briskly fry for 3–4 minutes until softened.

4 Add the bean sprouts and, continually stirring, cook briskly for about 1–2 minutes.

5 Meanwhile, warm the tortilla wraps as directed on the pack.

6 Spoon some of the pork mixture into the middle of each wrap and fold to contain the filling. Serve immediately, with salad leaves.

day 13

It's probably the weekend again, but this one shouldn't test your willpower too much. Partly because you've got only one more day on the plan to go, but also because now that you know how satisfied eating the GI way leaves you – and how energized you feel and how healthy you look while you follow its principles – there's no reason to cheat!

food

breakfast

glass of red grapefruit juice
150 ml (¼ pint)

boiled egg and slice of granary toast

ALTERNATIVE
bowl of porridge
Made using 3 tablespoons rolled oats and 200 ml (7 fl oz) water or skimmed milk. Top with a small banana.

snack

apple

lunch

chunky nut roast
(see page 80)

ALTERNATIVE
bought salad (under 300 calories) with grilled chicken and low-fat dressing

dessert

banana

snack

handful of plain peanuts and raisins
25 g (1 oz)

dinner

quick and easy risotto

Sweat sliced onions in a spray of olive oil in a large frying pan and add a selection of vegetables, such as red peppers, mushrooms and celery. Soften, then add 75 g (3 oz) cooked basmati rice, 50 g (2 oz) cooked chicken, peas and beans, 1 teaspoon tomato purée, oregano and some water. Continue to cook until the water has evaporated and the vegetables are cooked.

ALTERNATIVE

pizza

Top a small 17½ cm (7 inch) thin-crust pizza base with 2 tablespoons tomato pizza topping, 25 g (1 oz) low-fat grated cheese and unlimited chopped onions. Serve with a large side salad of red pepper, broccoli florets and 1 tablespoon sweetcorn.

dessert

wholegrain pancakes with cherries
(see page 81)

fit

Exercise doesn't need to involve shorts and trainers: gardening is a great calorie-burner and muscle-toner. If you've got a garden, head out there today and do some tidying – digging, weeding and mowing the lawn (with a manual mower) are the best calorie-burners.

fact

Watch the salt content of foods such as porridge oats and other cereals – some are saltier than sea water. In an ideal world you should not eat more than 6 g (⅕ oz) of salt a day: that's 2,400 mg of sodium. Check the labels of the foods that you choose carefully.

feel good

Spend a few minutes today reading the 'What's On' section of your local paper and booking tickets for something next week. Anticipation has been shown to increase the levels of endorphins (the same mood-boosting hormones released when you exercise), which will help to keep you feeling good next week when you're off the plan – and, hopefully, will prevent you reaching for comfort foods to cheer yourself up.

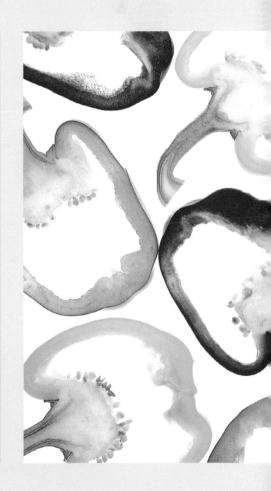

chunky nut roast

preparation: 15 minutes | **cooking:** 45 minutes | **serves:** 4

2 leeks, sliced

2 celery sticks, sliced

125 g (4 oz) chickpeas, cooked and roughly mashed

125 g (4 oz) brown rice, cooked

50 g (2 oz) mixed nuts, roughly chopped

2 teaspoons yeast extract

1 teaspoon chopped fresh mixed herbs

2 eggs, beaten

5 g (¼ oz) low-fat spread

20 g (¾ oz) dried breadcrumbs

salt and pepper

steamed broccoli and carrots, to serve

nutritional values per serving
Kcals **240 (1006 kJ)**
Protein **12.8 g**
Carb **21.2 g**
Sodium **576 mg**
Fat **12.2 g**
Sat. fat **2.3 g**
GI **Low**

1 Simmer the leeks and celery with a little water in a pan until soft. Allow to cool slightly.

2 Put the leeks and celery with the chickpeas, rice, nuts, yeast extract, herbs and pepper into a bowl and mix. Then add the eggs and combine.

3 Line a 450 g (14½ oz) loaf tin with nonstick paper, grease well with low-fat spread and sprinkle with the breadcrumbs. Spoon the mixture into the tin and level.

4 Bake uncovered in a preheated oven, 190°C (375°F), Gas Mark 5, for 45 minutes until set.

5 Serve in slices with steamed broccoli and carrots.

wholegrain pancakes with cherries

preparation: 10 minutes plus standing | **cooking:** 16 minutes | **serves:** 4

25 g (1 oz) wholegrain or wholemeal flour

25 g (1 oz) plain flour

1 egg, lightly beaten

75 ml (3 fl oz) skimmed milk

1 tablespoon vegetable oil

fresh or canned cherries

low-fat natural yogurt and cinnamon, to serve

1 Sift the flours and add the egg and milk, stirring to make a batter the consistency of single cream. Add extra milk if the batter seems too thick, or extra flour if it seems too thin.

2 Allow to stand in a covered bowl in the refrigerator for 1 hour.

3 Heat the oil in a small nonstick frying pan. Pour in a small amount of mixture and allow the mixture to run evenly over the base of the pan by lifting and turning it.

4 Cook on one side. Toss or lift and turn with a fish slice to cook the other side. Repeat with the remaining mixture to make 8 thin pancakes. Keep the pancakes warm as they are made.

5 Stew cherries in a pan with a little water. If using cherries canned in syrup, rinse off the syrup first by washing the cherries in a sieve under a tap.

6 Top the pancakes with the stewed cherries and serve with natural yogurt and a sprinkling of cinnamon.

tip

This recipe can be varied by using other fruit, such as apples or pears. Or why not try a savoury filling?

nutritional values per serving
Kcals **93 (369 kJ)**
Protein **3.8 g**
Carb **9.7 g**
Sodium **29 g**
Fat **4.6 g**
Sat. fat **0.8 g**
GI **Low**

day 14

This is it, the last official day of your diet, and hopefully you've lost all the weight you want to. If you'd still like to lose a little more weight, you can either repeat the diet (using some of the recipe adaptation tips) or use the charts on pages 110–125 to help you devise your own low-GI menus. Try to keep to around 1,500 calories a day for women and 2,000 calories for men.

food

breakfast

glass of apple juice
150 ml (¼ pint)

bowl of porridge
Made using 3 tablespoons rolled oats and 200 ml (7 fl oz) water or skimmed milk.

ALTERNATIVE
poached egg and toast
Serve the egg with a slice of toasted sourdough, soy/linseed or granary bread and grilled tomatoes.

snack

sunflower seeds
25 g (1 oz)

lunch

lemon and lime chicken with roasted vegetables
(see page 85)

ALTERNATIVE
roast vegetarian sausages and vegetables
2 roasted vegetarian sausages served with apple sauce, a mixture of 175 g (6 oz) dry-roasted potatoes in their skins and sweet potatoes, carrots, peas and Savoy cabbage.

dessert

red and green fruit salad
(see page 84)

snack

low-fat ice cream
50 g (2 oz)

dinner

mushroom omelette

Made with 2 eggs and served with a small wholemeal pitta bread and a large salad of leaves, sliced peppers, grated carrots and a handful of mint tossed in lemon juice.

ALTERNATIVE
pork stir-fry

Add a small (125 g/4 oz) grilled and sliced pork steak to a vegetable stir-fry made from a pack of stir-fry vegetables or a selection of mangetout, red and white onions, bean sprouts, noodles, oyster mushrooms, cherry tomatoes and courgettes. Serve in a small wholemeal pitta bread.

dessert

2 pineapple rings and a handful of cherries

fact

Remember that by losing weight you've not only helped yourself look better, but you've also lowered your risk of developing problems such as heart disease, diabetes and many cancers. Good for you!

fit

Why not make an appointment to go and see your local gym today? Most gyms will give you at least one trial session to see if you like it. At worst you'll get to do an hour of exercise – for example, trying a new class or testing out a strength-training regime such as weight training; at best you'll love it, join up and make exercise a part of your life from now on. Go on, give it a try.

feel good

Take a look at the size of the portions on your plate today – and memorize them. Portion control isn't just the easiest way to keep off the weight that you've lost for longer; it's also, according to many experts, potentially the key to a longer life. Researchers studying the diets of the Okinawan people (thought to be the longest-lived race on Earth) have discovered that their small portions mean they eat about 1,500 calories a day (close to what you've been on for the last two weeks). If you stick to small portions it will prevent overtaxing your digestion, which can lead to fatigue, bloating and belly ache.

red and green fruit salad

preparation: 10 minutes | **serves:** 4

4 kiwifruit

2 dessert apples, left unpeeled

1 pink grapefruit

handful of seedless green grapes, halved

4 tablespoons red berries

8 tablespoons low-sugar cranberry juice

low-fat natural yogurt, to serve

1 Slice the kiwifruit and apples and segment the grapefruit.

2 Mix in with the rest of the fruit and pour the cranberry juice over.

3 Serve with low-fat yogurt, allowing 75 g (3 oz) or about ½ pot per person.

nutritional values per serving
Kcals **74 (kJ 311)**
Protein **1.5 g**
Carb **16.6 g**
Sodium **6 mg**
Fat **0.5 g**
Sat. fat **0 g**
GI **Low**

tip

This easy recipe is also wonderful at breakfast time, and a very healthy way to start your day. You can alter the colour combination by changing the fruits used.

lemon and lime chicken with roasted vegetables

preparation: 10 minutes | **cooking:** 1½ hours | **serves:** 4

1.5 kg (3 lb) chicken

3 lemons, 1 sliced

2 limes, 1 sliced

1 tablespoon vegetable oil

4 sweet potatoes, peeled and cut into chunks

4 courgettes, cut into chunks

2 onions, cut into chunks

1 large red pepper, cored, deseeded and cut into chunks

chicken gravy, to serve

1 Wash the chicken. Place 1 whole lemon inside. Slit the skin and insert the lemon and lime slices under the skin over the breast.

2 Place in a lightly greased baking tray.

3 Cover with foil and roast in a preheated oven, 190°C (375°F), Gas Mark 5, for 1⅓–1½ hours or until cooked. Remove the foil for the last 5 minutes and spoon the meat juices over. Check that the chicken is cooked – the juices

should run clear when a skewer is inserted through the thickest part of the leg and breast.

4 Cook the vegetables at the same time as the chicken. Put the oil in a baking dish. Add the vegetable chunks and squeeze the remaining lemon and lime over the top. Roast above the chicken for 1 hour.

5 Serve the chicken and vegetables with the gravy.

nutritional values per serving

Kcals **486 (kJ 2024)**

Protein **36.4 g**

Carb **25.6 g**

Sodium **150 g**

Fat **27.0 g**

Sat. fat **7.0 g**

GI **Low**

FIT

Exercise is an important part of any weight-loss effort — in fact, new research from Duke University Medical Center in the United States found that the average non-exerciser gains 1.8 kg (4 lb) a year because of the calories they're not burning off by doing any activity. So to get optimum results from the 14-day diet programme you're going to need to do a little bit of exercise.

If you've never exercised before, this might not be good news. But remember that exercise on a low-GI eating plan like this has been scientifically proven to feel easier than normal. All that slow-releasing glucose in your system is giving you the fuel you need to work out with less fatigue than usual; and burning more fat when you exercise after a low-GI meal means that any workout you do is more productive. Bearing these two facts in mind, here's exactly what you should be doing.

exercise beginner

On the next few pages you'll find a simple toning programme that will help tighten and firm your muscles from head to toe. Each day you do a different workout to prevent your muscles getting tired. At the end of the week you start again with the first set of exercises — moving to the more advanced options if you feel up to it. Ideally, you should also do at least two of the daily 'fit' tasks from the 14-day plan (see pages 30–85) each week; and/or choose one of the exercises suggested on pages 104–107 and carry it out for 30 minutes twice a week.

middle ground

If you already work out, you can power up your workout: either start with the more advanced options, repeating the same workout again during the second week, or replace it with your normal weights programme at the gym. You can also do a 'fit' task at least five times a week, and/or choose one of the exercises suggested on pages 104–107 and carry it out for 30–60 minutes three to five times a week.

super-fit

If you're already a regular exerciser, doing just one set of toning exercises a day might not be challenging enough. Either replace them with your normal weights programme at the gym or, if you don't usually strength-train, carry out the suggested exercise plan each day, but combine two or three sets of exercises, using the advanced options. The next day choose two or three different sets to ensure that you're resting the muscles you worked yesterday. Repeat this approach for the next 14 days. In terms of aerobic work, you can complete a 'fit' task each day, and/or choose one of the exercises suggested on pages 104–107 and carry it out for 30–60 minutes five times a week.

safe exercise is happy exercise

The exercises here can easily be done at home, with no special equipment except one simple dumbbell that you'll find at any sports store. However, do wear trainers, as they give your ankles some support. Each day offers an individual warm-up exercise that will help reduce the risk of injury, but ideally you should also walk or jog (depending on your fitness level) around the garden, up and down stairs or even on the spot for five minutes before you start. Anyone who is very overweight or has health problems should consult their doctor or fitness professional before starting any exercise regime.

days 4 and 11

Back to working on those core postural muscles again – this time focusing on the back muscles, particularly those that run along the spine. Many of us ignore these in favour of toning our tummies or thighs, but if the back muscles are weak, the whole body hangs out of alignment, which leads to pouchy stomachs and saggy gluteus muscles (and the buttocks they hold up).

warm-up exercise
the curve

1 With your feet slightly apart and your hands on your thighs, bend your knees. Now curve your back, pulling in your stomach muscles as if someone has just punched you!

2 Flatten your back out again and press your buttocks out behind you. Repeat the curve-and-flatten technique five times.

1

2

toning exercise
the hyper-extension

This is an effective exercise for strengthening the muscles that run along the spine.

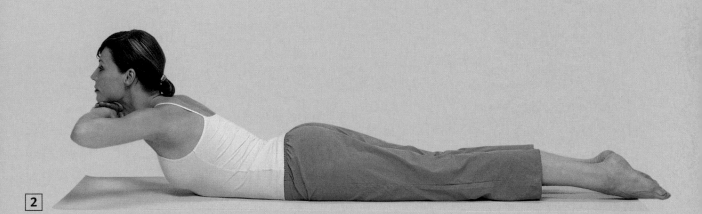

1 Lie on your front, with your arms resting on the floor in front of you and your head resting on your arms.

2 Now lift your head and hands up off the floor, and raise your shoulders and chest upwards. Hold this lift for five breaths, before returning your upper body to the floor. Repeat the exercise ten times in week one; in week two either add five more repetitions, or relax after the first set and then repeat the exercise again ten times.

to finish

Spend five minutes jumping on the spot to boost your oxygen intake.

days 6 and 13

The backs of the arms are another area that is frequently ignored, but as your shoulders start to align into a better postural position, the backs of your arms can be pressed closer to your body and may actually start to look bigger than you would like them to. The good news is that a few simple exercises can have them tightened up and looking firmer in no time.

warm-up exercise
the side-shimmy

1 Stand with your legs wide apart and your arms extended out to each side, with palms facing back.

2 While bending your legs to one side and then the other, bend and straighten your arms, bringing your hands into your chest and out again. Do this 15 times, getting more vigorous each time.

toning exercise
the triceps trial

When you do this exercise, wedge your chair against a wall to make sure that it doesn't slip when you press against it.

1 Sit on the edge of a chair or bench, with your hands on the edge of the seat and your feet flat on the floor. Now inch your buttocks off the chair, taking your weight on to your arms.

2 Lower your buttocks down towards the floor, then push with your arms to raise them up again. All the work here should be done by your arms, and not by your legs. Repeat up to ten times in week one; in week two take a rest after the first set, then repeat again, aiming to do eight to ten repetitions if you can.

to finish

Spend five minutes skipping (just like boxers do – you don't need a skipping rope) to boost your energy levels.

days 7 and 14

Finally it's time to work on the lower leg. Having and maintaining an erect posture hinges on having strength and correct positioning in the ankles, feet and knees. So even though you might not worry about how they look in a bikini, it's important not to ignore these areas. These exercises are good for your circulation and will also help you create leaner, more shapely calf muscles.

warm-up exercise
tiptoe through the tulips

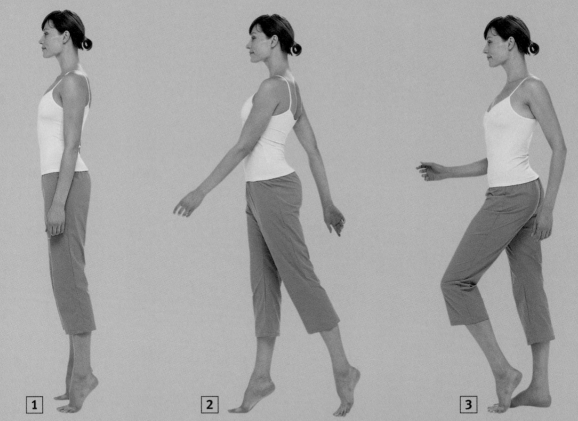

1 Stand on tiptoe and breathe normally to a count of five.

2 Walk on tiptoe from one side of the room to the other.

3 Now stand and press one heel to the floor and then the other. Raise and lower each heel in turn 10–15 times until your ankles and legs feel warm.

toning exercise
the jump

Don't look down as you do this series of jumps. Keep your eyes fixed straight ahead to help you with your balance.

1 Stand with your feet hip-width apart, then bend your knees and jump, swinging your arms as you do so. Aim to lift your feet right into the air and stretch them underneath you. Try to land on the balls of your feet and let the rest of your feet roll on to the floor as you land, bending your knees to absorb the shock.

2 Now repeat the exercise, but don't push yourself right off the floor – your toes should stay in contact with it. Repeat both exercises eight times, then rest and repeat a further three times in week one to shape the calves. In week two do 10–15 raises, again repeating them three times.

to finish

Spend five minutes lying flat on the floor with your feet raised on a bed or bench and your head lower than your feet to boost the blood flow to your brain and help reduce fluid retention in your lower legs.

Calories burned

Remember, the bigger the gap between the number of calories you eat each day and those you burn, the more weight you lose on a slimming regime. Every time you move you burn calories, but obviously some activities are better at this than others.

This chart explains how many calories a 68 kg (10 st 10 lb) woman will burn doing some common daily tasks or fitness activities; men and women who weigh more than this will burn more calories – to calculate exactly how many, divide the number of calories listed by 150, and then multiply it by your weight in pounds. Depending on your fitness level, you could replace any of your daily 'fit' tasks with 30–60 minutes of any of these activities.

ACTIVITY	CALORIES/KCAL PER 15 MINUTES	ACTIVITY	CALORIES/KCAL PER 15 MINUTES	ACTIVITY	CALORIES/KCAL PER 15 MINUTES
Aerobics	95	Cycling (outside – moderate)	158	Jogging	125
Aikido (intense)	158	Dancing (general)	70	Judo	158
Aqua aerobics	77	Darts	39	Kayaking (moderate)	79
Archery	55	Digging	100	Kick-boxing	158
Ashtanga yoga	100	Downhill skiing	79	Lawn mowing (push mower)	87
Badminton	71	Driving	27	Line-dancing	70
Basketball	95	Dusting	40	Mopping the floor	45
Bathing the dog	66	Fishing	63	Mountain biking	135
Billiards	39	Football	100	Moving furniture	90
Bowling	47	Gardening	80	Netball	95
Boxing	142	Golf (with cart)	45	Painting (interior)	71
Canoeing	120	Golf (without cart)	60	Papering walls	48
Carpentry	55	Gymnastics	63	Pilates (light)	50
Carrying shopping	63	Hatha yoga	40	Pilates (moderate)	75
Cleaning the house	39	Hiking	95	Pilates (intense)	100
Climbing stairs	150	Hockey	100	Playing tag	80
Cooking	27	Ice hockey	130	Power-walking	103
Cricket	79	Ice skating (moderate)	75	Pushing a pushchair	39
Cross-country skiing	125	Indoor climbing	175	Raking leaves	72
Cycling (on an exercise bike)	79	Irish step-dancing	87	Resistance bands	75

ACTIVITY	CALORIES/KCAL PER 15 MINUTES	ACTIVITY	CALORIES/KCAL PER 15 MINUTES	ACTIVITY	CALORIES/KCAL PER 15 MINUTES
Rock-climbing	175	Squash (intense)	212	Toning tables	55
Rounders	79	Stairmaster machine	145	Treadmill running	140
Rowing (machine)	137	Standing	25	Treadmill running (on 5% incline)	160
Rowing (outside)	175	Step aerobics	140	Vacuuming	45
Rugby	158	Stretching	40	Volleyball	127
Sailing	47	Stripping wallpaper	48	Walking (normal pace)	55
Scrubbing the floor	87	Sweeping the floor	65	Walking (brisk)	63
Shopping	45	Sweeping the path	70	Washing dishes	45
Shovelling snow	106	Swimming (breaststroke)	95	Washing the car	64
Sit-ups	63	Swimming (butterfly)	175	Weight training	54
Skipping	175	Swimming (front crawl)	125	Window cleaning	45
Snorkelling	79	Tai chi	63	Windsurfing	50
Spinning class	160	Tennis (doubles)	95		
Sprinting	214	Tennis (singles)	160		

how hard is too hard?

The harder you do any activity, the more calories you'll burn. However, if you work out too hard for your fitness level, you'll get too tired to gain the maximum benefit. And you burn a higher proportion of fat if you work out at about 70 per cent of your maximum ability. So whenever you do any exercise on this plan (or generally in life) you should aim to be working at a level that feels like roughly six or seven out of ten. Or use the 'talk test' discussed briefly on page 55: you should be working hard enough to be able to speak in sentences, but should feel the need to take a break between them.

Fun activities

Still not convinced that working out is right for you? Then make your daily 'fit' task something fun. None of the activities below feels like exercise, but they all help you tone and burn calories. Go on – give one or two of them a try over the next 14 days.

archery
Burning 220 calories an hour, it's easy to see why archery creates firm arm muscles and helps sculpt a strong upper back. Other fitness boosts include dramatically improved posture and tightened tummy muscles. It won't help your aerobic fitness, though, so don't make it your only workout.

belly-dancing
Not only does it burn around 381 calories an hour, but it also helps tone the muscles of the stomach, waist, hips and thighs. Videos teaching the technique are available; or look in your local newspaper or at your local sports centre to see if classes are offered.

boogie-boarding
A great sport for anyone who lives near a beach. All you need is a small, light board; you then run into the waves and lie on the board to surf your way back in.

Running against the resistance of the water helps tone your legs, while staying on the board requires tight, toned tummy muscles.

dancing video games
These are played on a home games system and burn a staggering 600 calories an hour, if you get good at it. You stand on a mat with sensors and get your instructions onscreen as to what steps to do – and are scored for accuracy. Your local computer games store can tell you more about what you need to get started.

flamenco
Or salsa, or ballroom ... Dance classes are a gentle way for people who don't normally exercise to start improving their fitness, without the pressure of visiting a gym. They burn a minimum of 200 calories an hour, and you'll also slim your legs and improve your posture.

frisbee
This sport is even better for your body shape if you're bad at it – the more you run after the frisbee and reach over to pick it up, the more calories you burn (on average around 200 an hour). Jumping to catch the disc also causes rapid toning of buttocks and thighs.

horseriding
Burning around 280 calories an hour, riding firms up the thighs, buttocks and stomach. But the calorie-burning doesn't stop when you dismount; grooming a horse will burn around 200 calories in half an hour. If you've never ridden before, take a few lessons – if you're a natural, you'll be trotting in a month or less.

hula-hooping
If you want to flatten your tummy fast, this is the exercise for you. You have to hold in your

stomach muscles to keep the hoop rotating – and you'll burn about 300 calories an hour while having fun. For extra benefits, think about using a weighted hoop (available from sports stores) to intensify your workout.

in-line skating

This gives your heart and lungs a similar level of workout to running, but you don't feel as if you're working anything like as hard, because the wind helps keep you cool and there's no impact on your joints to cause pain. An hour's skate will burn 480 calories.

kite-flying

A great activity to do with children, stationary kite-flying will burn only 100 calories an hour. Get yourself a sports kite in a high wind, however, and that could increase to 250 calories as you twist and turn to catch the wind – and run (or at least walk briskly) to pick up your kite when it falls.

pedal-boating

You'll find pedal boats in local parks and, while they may look simple, they give you the same workout as sitting on a type of exercise bike called a recumbent and pedalling it on medium resistance. As a result you'll burn about 300 calories in an hour – and work your legs and buttock muscles.

playgrounding

Also known as 'playing with your children', this will have you clambering on the climbing frame, spinning the roundabout, pushing them on the swings and running round the playground as if you were six again. Burning around 350 calories an hour, this is another great way to involve your children in your fitness efforts.

snowboarding

You don't need to live near a mountain to do this – many indoor ski slopes offer lessons, too. It's said to be easier to learn than skiing (as both legs are on the same piece of equipment) and all you need to succeed is good balance. An hour's session will burn around 350 calories.

table tennis

A fast game of table tennis can be such a good workout that it's now being rebranded 'Killer Spin'. For most of us, though, it's just a nice way to have fun with the kids. The more you move around the table and reach for shots, the greater its fitness effects; you could expect to burn 250 calories in an hour-long tournament.

trampolining

Toning buttocks and thighs and speeding up the lymph system (which helps flush fluid and toxins out of the body), trampolining is one of those exercises where you don't realize how hard you're working because you're laughing so much. But you are working hard: manage 30 minutes and you'll burn 150–200 calories.

FOREVER

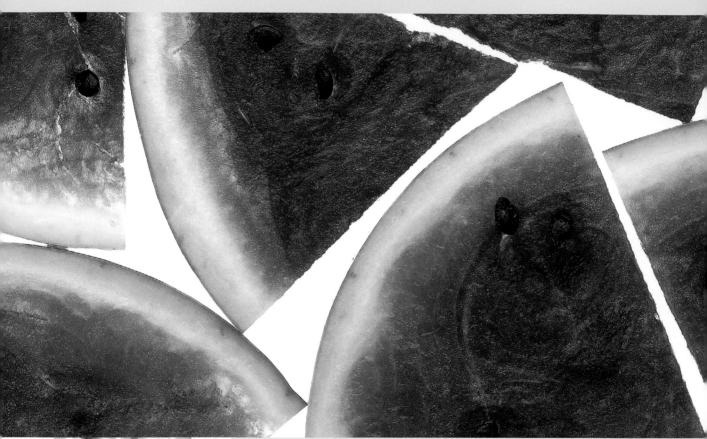

So that's it: your 14-day plan is finished, and hopefully you're thrilled with the results. What now? Well, if you've got more weight to lose, turn back to pages 24–25 for tips on how to adapt the diet for longer term weight loss or use the charts on the following pages to create your own eating plan. If you've achieved the weight loss you wanted, congratulations — you've taken the first step to that slimmer new you. So what exactly should you eat from now on to keep it that way?

low-GI for life

Many fast-fix weight-loss plans simply don't teach you what to eat once the weight has come off. This plan isn't like that. Because all the food groups are included, you don't feel as if you're missing out on things, and the inclusion of desserts and 'high-fat' foods like chocolate, nuts and seeds helps you appreciate that you can have higher calorie treats and still stay slim. So eating the low-GI way for life is relatively easy.

To determine exactly what you should eat, you can use two maintenance tools. The box on this page tells you how to adapt the GI pyramid from pages 20–21 to maintain your weight, and the charts on the following pages will help you mix and match your own eating choices to tailor that pyramid to your likes and dislikes. A few final facts will help you incorporate higher GI foods into your eating plan without adversely affecting your blood-sugar levels.

1 Try not to have more than one high-GI food a day. Two weeks of low-GI eating will have stabilized your blood-sugar levels and reduced the amount of insulin in your system. However, if you start overloading your system with high-GI foods, the situation will reverse, your energy levels will fall, and you could find yourself overeating and the weight going back on.

2 If you do eat a high-GI food, combining it with a low-GI food will reduce the speed at which the high-GI one converts to sugar. So if you treat yourself to some crusty French bread or mashed potato, eat it with a little fat, protein or a selection of vegetables to help lower the GI.

3 Keep portions of all carbohydrates sensible. The more of a particular food you eat, the more glucose is produced, so to avoid overloading your system keep portion sizes to those suggested on pages 22–23.

the GI maintenance pyramid

The GI pyramid (see page 21) indicates the overall proportions of the different food groups that you should eat each day when you're trying to diet. However, it's a bit restrictive once you've lost the weight, so you can amend it as follows:

• The high-GI, low-nutrient foods in the top section can be enjoyed 1–2 times a week.

• The high-GI, higher-nutrient foods in the second layer can be eaten once a day.

• The next sections (nuts and seeds, dairy and protein foods) should remain the same.

• You can now increase the carbohydrates you eat and incorporate up to two portions of medium-GI foods, such as couscous or brown rice. Women should stick to 6–8 servings, while men can eat up to 11 (remember that any high-GI carbs should be included in this total).

• Fruit and vegetables should stay the same, aiming for at least 5 portions a day — ideally in a 3:2, vegetable: fruit ratio.

GI chart

This chart shows the energy content of foods per 100 g (3½ oz) as kcal (kilocalories) and kJ (kilojoules).The GI value of foods is also shown, together with whether with the food in question is high, medium or low in GI terms.It should be noted that the GI values can vary between varieties of fruits and vegetables and different manufacturers, and according to the way in which items are cooked. The value for both cooked and raw items has been given if they are commonly served as such. Remember that where possible it is better to steam vegetables as this helps to retain the vitamin content. The values given here remain the same for boiling and steaming.

	KCAL	KJ	GI VALUE		KCAL	KJ	GI VALUE
A				**B**			
Alfalfa	24	100	1 low	**Bacon,** back rasher, grilled	287	1194	0 low
Anchovies, canned in oil	191	798	0 low	**Bacon,** back rasher, reduced salt, grilled	282	1172	0 low
Apple	47	199	38 low	**Bacon,** streaky rasher, grilled	337	1400	0 low
Apple juice, unsweetened	38	164	40 low				
Apricots, canned in juice	34	147	64 med	**Bagel,** white	273	1161	72 high
Apricots, dried	188	802	30 low	**Baked beans**	84	355	48 low
Apricots, fresh	31	134	57 med	**Baked beans,** reduced sugar and salt	73	311	48 low
Artichoke, boiled	18	77	1 low				
Artichoke, canned	28	119	1 low	**Baked potato**	136	581	85 high
Asparagus, steamed	26	110	1 low	**Baking powder**	157	693	0 low
Aubergine, fried	302	1246	1 low	**Banana**	95	403	52 low
Avocado	190	784	1 low	**Barley, pearl,** boiled	120	510	25 low
				Basmati rice, boiled	138	587	58 med
				Bean sprouts, raw	31	131	1 low

	KCAL	KJ	GI VALUE		KCAL	KJ	GI VALUE
Bean sprouts, stir-fried	72	298	1 low	**Split peas,** soaked and boiled	126	538	32 low
				Soya beans, boiled	141	590	20 low

BEANS AND PULSES

	KCAL	KJ	GI VALUE
Baked beans	84	355	48 low
Baked beans, reduced sugar and salt	73	311	48 low
Black-eyed beans, soaked and boiled	116	494	42 low
Broad beans, steamed	48	204	61 med
Buckwheat, boiled	364	1522	54 low
Butter beans, canned	77	327	36 low
Butter beans, soaked and boiled	103	437	31 low
Chickpeas, canned	115	487	42 low
Chickpeas, soaked and boiled	121	512	28 low
Green beans, steamed	25	108	1 low
Green beans, raw	24	99	1 low
Haricot beans, soaked and boiled	95	406	33 low
Kidney beans, canned	100	424	36 low
Kidney beans, soaked and boiled	100	424	28 low
Lentils, green, canned	64	273	48 low
Lentils, green, soaked and boiled	105	446	30 low
Lentils, red, soaked and boiled	100	424	26 low

	KCAL	KJ	GI VALUE
Beef, corned, canned	205	860	0 low
Beef, grillsteaks, grilled	305	1268	0 low
Beef, rump steak, lean fried	183	770	0 low
Beef, rump steak, lean grilled	177	745	0 low
Beef, stewing steak stewed	185	777	0 low
Beefburgers, 99% meat, grilled	326	1353	0 low
Beetroot, boiled	46	195	80 high

BISCUITS AND CRACKERS

	KCAL	KJ	GI VALUE
Digestive biscuits	465	1956	59 med
Oatcakes	412	1737	54 low
Rice cakes, white	374	1591	82 high
Shortbread	509	2133	64 med
Black-eyed beans, soaked and boiled	116	494	42 low
Bran cereal, noodle-shaped	270	1144	34 low
Bran cereal, flakes	330	1406	74 high

BREADS, CAKES AND PASTRY

	KCAL	KJ	GI VALUE
Bagel, white	273	1161	72 high

	KCAL	KJ	GI VALUE		KCAL	KJ	GI VALUE
Chocolate cake	456	1908	38 low	Rice cereal, plain	382	1628	82 high
Croissant	373	1563	67 med	Weetabix	352	1498	69 med
Crumpet	177	753	69 med	Wheat cereal	89	376	0 low
Fruit bread	295	1256	47 low				
Fruit cake	371	1561	54 low	Broad beans, steamed	48	204	61 med
Granary bread	237	1005	61 med	Broccoli, green, boiled	24	100	1 low
Pancakes	302	1265	67 med	Broccoli, green, raw	33	138	1 low
Pastry	451	1884	59 med	Brussels sprouts, steamed	35	153	1 low
Pitta bread, white	255	1084	57 med	Buckwheat, boiled	364	1522	54 low
Pretzels	381	1596	83 high	Butter	744	3059	0 low
Rye bread, no grains	219	932	51 low	Butter beans, canned	77	327	36 low
Rye/pumpernickel bread, with grains	219	932	41 low	Butter beans, soaked and cooked	103	437	31 low
Scones, plain	364	1530	92 high				

	KCAL	KJ	GI VALUE
Soy/linseed bread	252	1070	41 low
Sponge cake	467	1951	46 low
Waffles	334	1401	76 high
White bread	235	1002	70 high
Wholemeal bread	217	922	77 high

BREAKFAST CEREALS

	KCAL	KJ	GI VALUE
Bran cereal, noodle-shaped	270	1144	34 low
Bran cereal, flakes	330	1406	74 high
Chocolate rice cereal	383	1632	77 high
Cornflakes	376	1601	77 high
Muesli, Swiss	363	1540	56 med
Porridge oats, dried	401	1698	42 low

C

	KCAL	KJ	GI VALUE
Cabbage, steamed	16	67	1 low
Cabbage, raw	26	109	1 low
Camembert cheese	290	1205	0 low
Carrots, steamed	24	100	31 low
Carrots, raw	35	146	49 low
Cauliflower, boiled	28	117	1 low
Cauliflower, raw	34	142	1 low
Celery, steamed	8	34	0 low
Celery, raw	7	30	0 low
Cheddar cheese	416	1725	0 low
Cheddar cheese, low-fat	273	1141	0 low

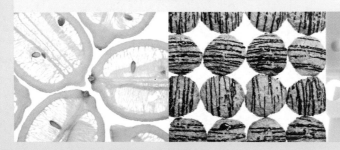

CHEESES

	KCAL	KJ	GI VALUE
Camembert	290	1205	0 low
Cheddar	416	1725	0 low
Cheddar, low-fat	273	1141	0 low
Cottage cheese	101	423	0 low
Cottage cheese, low-fat	79	334	0 low
Cream cheese	439	1807	0 low
Edam	341	1416	0 low
Edam, low-fat	229	957	0 low
Feta	250	1037	0 low
Mozzarella	257	1067	0 low
Parmesan	415	1729	0 low
Stilton	410	1698	0 low
Cherries	48	203	22 low
Chicken, breast, no skin grilled	148	626	0 low
Chicken, drumsticks roasted	185	775	0 low
Chicken, meat and skin roasted	216	912	0 low
Chicken, strips, stir-fried	161	677	0 low
Chickpeas, canned	115	487	42 low
Chickpeas, soaked and boiled	121	512	28 low
Chocolate, milk	520	2177	42 low
Chocolate, plain	510	2137	41 low
Chocolate cake	456	1908	38 low

	KCAL	KJ	GI VALUE
Chocolate mousse	149	627	37 low
Chocolate mousse, low-fat	123	518	31 low
Chocolate rice cereal	383	1632	77 high
Cockles, boiled	53	226	0 low
Coconut oil	899	3696	0 low
Cod fillet, baked	96	408	0 low
Coffee, black	0	0	0 low
Cola	41	174	53 low
Cola, diet	0	0	0 low
Coley, steamed	105	444	0 low
Condensed milk	333	1406	61 med
Corn chips	459	1927	42 low
Corned beef, canned	205	860	0 low
Cornflakes	376	1601	77 high
Cottage cheese	101	423	0 low
Cottage cheese, low-fat	79	334	0 low
Courgette, steamed	19	81	1 low
Courgette, fried	62	265	1 low
Courgette, raw	18	74	1 low
Couscous, cooked	227	950	65 med
Crab, canned in brine	77	326	0 low
Crab meat, boiled	128	535	0 low
Cranberry juice	61	259	52 low
Cream cheese	439	1807	0 low
Crisps, potato	530	2215	57 med

	KCAL	KJ	GI VALUE
Croissant	373	1563	67 med
Crumpet	177	753	69 med
Cucumber	10	40	1 low
Curly kale, steamed	24	100	1 low
Curly kale, raw	33	140	1 low
Custard powder, made with skimmed milk	95	404	35 low
Custard powder, made with whole milk	118	492	35 low

D

DAIRY PRODUCTS

	KCAL	KJ	GI VALUE
Condensed milk	333	1406	61 med
Custard powder, made with skimmed milk	95	404	35 low
Custard powder, made with whole milk	118	492	35 low
Ice cream, full-fat	177	741	61 med
Ice cream, low-fat	119	499	50 low
Skimmed milk	32	136	32 low
Soya milk	32	132	36 low
Soya yogurt	72	305	50 low
Whole milk	66	274	31 low
Yogurt, low-fat	56	237	33 low
Yogurt, low-fat, fruit	78	331	31 low
Yogurt, virtually fat-free, diet	54	230	20 low

	KCAL	KJ	GI VALUE
Dates, dried	270	1151	103 high

	KCAL	KJ	GI VALUE
Diet cola	0	0	0 low
Digestive biscuits	465	1956	59 med

DRINKS

	KCAL	KJ	GI VALUE
Apple juice, unsweetened	38	164	40 low
Coffee, black, no sugar	0	0	0 low
Cola	41	174	53 low
Cola, diet	0	0	0 low
Cranberry juice	61	259	52 low
Grapefruit juice, unsweetened	33	140	48 low
Orange juice, unsweetened	36	153	53 low
Pineapple juice, unsweetened	41	177	46 low
Tea, black	0	0	0 low
Tea, herbal	0	0	0 low
Tomato juice, no added sugar	14	62	38 low
Water	0	0	0 low

	KCAL	KJ	GI VALUE
Duck, crispy Chinese	331	1375	0 low
Duck, meat and skin roasted	388	1603	0 low
Duck, meat only, roasted	195	815	0 low

E

	KCAL	KJ	GI VALUE
Edam cheese	341	1416	0 low

	KCAL	KJ	GI VALUE		KCAL	KJ	GI VALUE
Edam cheese, low-fat	229	957	0 low	**Kippers,** grilled	161	667	0 low
Eels, jellied	98	406	0 low	**Lemon sole,** steamed	91	384	0 low
Egg noodles, boiled	62	264	46 low	**Lobster,** boiled	103	435	0 low
Egg white	6	153	0 low	**Mackerel,** fresh, fried	272	1130	0 low
Eggs	151	627	0 low	**Monkfish,** grilled	96	407	0 low
Eggs, boiled	151	627	0 low	**Mussels,** boiled, no shells	28	119	0 low
Eggs, fried	179	745	0 low	**Mussels,** boiled, with shells	104	440	0 low
Eggs, omelette, cheese	271	1121	0 low	**Oysters,** raw	65	275	0 low
Eggs, omelette, plain	195	808	0 low	**Plaice,** grilled	96	404	0 low
Eggs, poached	147	612	0 low	**Prawns,** peeled and boiled	99	418	0 low
Eggs, scrambled	257	1062	0 low	**Salmon,** canned in brine	153	644	0 low
				Salmon, canned in oil	153	644	0 low
F				**Salmon,** smoked	142	598	0 low
Fennel, boiled	11	47	1 low	**Salmon,** steamed	194	812	0 low
Fennel, raw	12	50	1 low	**Sardines,** canned in oil	220	918	0 low
Feta cheese	250	1037	0 low	**Sardines,** fresh, grilled	195	815	0 low
Figs, dried	227	967	61 med	**Scallops,** steamed	118	501	0 low
				Shrimps, canned in brine	94	398	0 low
FISH AND SHELLFISH				**Shrimps,** frozen	73	310	0 low
Anchovies, canned in oil	191	798	0 low	**Sole fillet,** steamed	91	384	0 low
Cockles, boiled	53	226	0 low	**Swordfish,** grilled	139	583	0 low
Cod fillet, poached	94	396	0 low	**Trout fillet,** grilled	135	565	0 low
Coley, steamed	105	444	0 low	**Tuna,** canned in brine	99	422	0 low
Crab, canned in brine	77	326	0 low	**Tuna,** canned in oil	189	794	0 low
Crab meat, boiled	128	535	0 low				
Haddock, steamed	89	378	0 low				
Halibut, grilled	121	513	0 low				

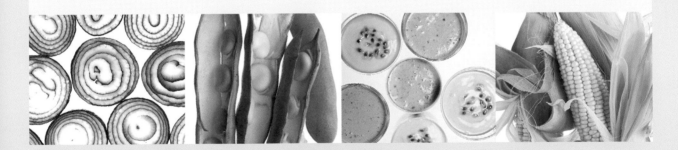

	KCAL	KJ	GI VALUE
Frankfurter, ready-cooked	287	1189	0 low

FRUIT

	KCAL	KJ	GI VALUE
Apple	47	199	38 low
Apple juice, unsweetened	38	164	40 low
Apricots, canned in juice	34	147	64 med
Apricots, dried	188	802	30 low
Apricots, fresh	31	134	57 med
Avocado	190	784	1 low
Banana	95	403	52 low
Cherries	48	203	22 low
Figs, dried	227	967	61 med
Fruit cocktail, canned in syrup	57	244	55 low
Grapefruit	30	126	25 low
Grapefruit juice, unsweetened	33	140	48 low
Grapes, red	60	257	53 low
Grapes, white	60	257	53 low
Kiwifruit	49	207	53 low
Mango	57	245	51 low
Orange	37	158	42 low
Orange juice, unsweetened	36	153	53 low
Papaya	36	153	56 med
Peaches, canned in juice	39	165	40 low
Pears, canned in juice	33	141	45 low

	KCAL	KJ	GI VALUE
Pineapple, canned in juice	47	200	46 low
Pineapple, fresh	41	176	66 med
Pineapple juice, unsweetened	41	177	46 low
Plums	34	145	34 low
Prunes	141	601	29 low
Raisins	272	1159	64 med
Rhubarb, stewed	7	30	0 low
Sultanas	275	1171	56 med
Tomato juice, no added sugar	14	62	38 low
Watermelon, no skin	31	133	72 high
Fruit bread	295	1256	47 low
Fruit cake	371	1561	54 low
Fruit cocktail, canned in syrup	57	244	55 low

G

	KCAL	KJ	GI VALUE
Gammon steak, fat removed, boiled	204	851	0 low
Gelatine	338	1435	0 low
Ghee	895	3693	0 low
Goose, meat and skin roasted	301	1252	0 low
Granary bread	237	1005	61 med
Grapefruit	30	126	25 low
Grapefruit juice, unsweetened	33	140	48 low

	KCAL	KJ	GI VALUE
Grapes, red	60	257	53 low
Grapes, white	60	257	53 low
Green beans, steamed	25	108	1 low
Green beans, raw	24	99	1 low

H

	KCAL	KJ	GI VALUE
Haddock, steamed	89	378	0 low
Halibut, grilled	121	513	0 low
Ham	107	451	0 low
Haricot beans, soaked and boiled	95	406	33 low
Herbal tea	0	0	0 low
Herbs, dried	181	760	1 low
Herbs, fresh	34	141	1 low
Heart, lamb, roasted	226	944	0 low
Honey	288	1229	55 low
Hummus	187	781	6 low

I

	KCAL	KJ	GI VALUE
Ice cream, full-fat	177	741	61 med
Ice cream, low-fat	119	499	50 low
Instant mashed potato	57	245	86 high

J

	KCAL	KJ	GI VALUE
Jam, apricot, reduced sugar	123	523	55 low
Jam, strawberry	261	1114	56 med

K

	KCAL	KJ	GI VALUE
Kidney, lamb, fried	188	784	0 low
Kidney, ox, stewed	138	579	0 low
Kidney, pig stewed and fried	153	641	0 low
Kidney beans, canned	100	424	36 low
Kidney beans, soaked and boiled	100	424	28 low
Kippers, grilled	161	667	0 low
Kiwifruit	49	207	53 low

L

	KCAL	KJ	GI VALUE
Lamb, kebab, grilled	288	1199	0 low
Lamb, lean, roasted	203	853	0 low
Lamb, loin chop, lean grilled	213	892	0 low
Lamb, loin chop, with fat grilled	277	1150	0 low
Lamb, mince, stewed	208	870	0 low
Lard	891	3663	0 low
Leeks, steamed	21	87	1 low
Lemon sole, steamed	91	384	0 low
Lentils, green canned	64	273	48 low
Lentils, green soaked and boiled	105	446	30 low
Lentils, red soaked and boiled	100	424	26 low
Lettuce, round	14	59	1 low

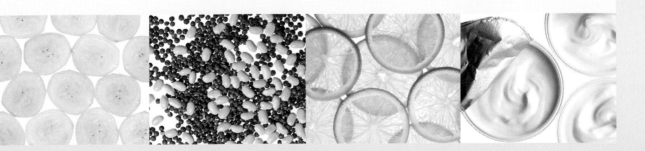

	KCAL	KJ	GI VALUE
Lettuce, iceberg	13	53	1 low
Liver, calf, fried	188	784	0 low
Liver, chicken, fried	169	705	0 low
Liver, lamb, fried	237	989	0 low
Liver, ox, stewed	198	831	0 low
Liver pâté	348	1437	0 low
Lobster, boiled	103	435	0 low
Low-fat spread, 40% fat	390	1608	0 low
Low-fat spread, 75% fat	680	2795	0 low

M

	KCAL	KJ	GI VALUE
Mackerel, fresh, fried	272	1130	0 low
Margarine	718	2954	0 low
Mangetout, steamed	26	111	1 low
Mangetout, stir-fried	71	298	1 low
Mangetout, raw	32	136	1 low
Mango	57	245	51 low
Marrow, boiled	9	38	1 low
Mashed potato, instant	57	245	86 high
Meat extract	179	760	0 low

MEATS

	KCAL	KJ	GI VALUE
Bacon, back rasher grilled	287	1194	0 low
Bacon, back rasher reduced salt, grilled	282	1172	0 low
Bacon, streaky rasher grilled	337	1400	0 low

	KCAL	KJ	GI VALUE
Beef, grillsteaks, grilled	305	1268	0 low
Beef, rump steak, lean fried	183	770	0 low
Beef, rump steak, lean grilled	177	745	0 low
Beef, stewing steak stewed	185	613	0 low
Beef, topside, lean and fat roasted	222	930	0 low
Beefburgers, 99% meat, grilled	326	1353	0 low
Beef, corned, canned	205	860	0 low
Gammon steak, fat removed, boiled	204	851	0 low
Ham	107	451	0 low
Kidney, lamb, fried	188	784	0 low
Kidney, ox, stewed	138	579	0 low
Kidney, pig, stewed and fried	153	641	0 low
Lamb, kebab, grilled	288	1199	0 low
Lamb, lean, roasted	203	853	0 low
Lamb, loin chop, lean grilled	213	892	0 low
Lamb, loin chop, with fat grilled	277	1150	0 low
Lamb, mince, stewed	208	870	0 low
Liver, calf, fried	188	784	0 low
Liver, chicken, fried	169	705	0 low
Liver, lamb, fried	237	989	0 low
Liver, ox, stewed	198	831	0 low

	KCAL	KJ	GI VALUE
Liver pâté	348	1437	0 low
Pork, belly, grilled	320	1332	0 low
Pork, chop, lean and fat roasted	301	1256	0 low
Pork, fillet strips stir-fried	182	764	0 low
Pork, leg, lean and fat roasted	182	765	0 low
Pork, loin chop, lean grilled	184	774	0 low
Pork, steak, lean and fat grilled	198	832	0 low
Sausages, pork, grilled	294	1221	28 low
Veal, escalope, fried	196	825	0 low
Veal, escalope, roasted	230	960	0 low
Venison, roasted	165	698	0 low

MILKS

	KCAL	KJ	GI VALUE
Condensed milk	333	1406	61 med
Skimmed milk	32	136	32 low
Soya milk	32	132	36 low
Soya yogurt	72	305	50 low
Whole milk	65	274	31 low

	KCAL	KJ	GI VALUE
Mint, fresh	43	181	1 low
Monkfish, grilled	96	407	0 low
Mozzarella cheese	257	1067	0 low
Muesli, Swiss	363	1540	56 med
Mushrooms, fried	157	645	1 low

	KCAL	KJ	GI VALUE
Mushrooms, raw	13	55	1 low
Mussels, boiled, no shells	28	119	0 low
Mussels, boiled, with shells	104	440	0 low
Mustard, wholegrain	140	584	1 low
Mustard and cress	13	56	1 low

N

	KCAL	KJ	GI VALUE
New potatoes, canned, reheated and drained	66	281	65 med
New potatoes, unpeeled, boiled in their skins	75	321	76 high

O

	KCAL	KJ	GI VALUE
Oatcakes	412	1737	54 low

OILS AND FATS

	KCAL	KJ	GI VALUE
Butter	744	3059	0 low
Coconut oil	899	3696	0 low
Ghee	895	3693	0 low
Lard	891	3663	0 low
Low-fat spread, 40% fat	390	1608	0 low
Low-fat spread, 75% fat	680	2795	0 low
Margarine	718	2954	0 low
Olive oil	899	3696	0 low
Peanut/groundnut oil	899	3696	0 low
Sesame oil	899	3696	0 low
Sunflower oil	899	3696	0 low
Vegetable oil	899	3696	0 low

	KCAL	KJ	GI VALUE
Okra, boiled	28	119	1 low
Okra, fried	269	1122	1 low
Olive oil	899	3696	0 low
Omelette, cheese	271	1121	0 low
Omelette, plain	195	808	0 low
Onions, fried	164	684	0 low
Onions, raw	36	150	0 low
Orange	37	158	42 low
Orange juice, unsweetened	36	153	53 low
Oysters, raw	65	275	0 low

P

	KCAL	KJ	GI VALUE
Pancakes	302	1265	67 med
Papaya	36	153	56 med
Parmesan cheese	415	1729	0 low
Parsley, fresh	34	141	1 low

PASTA, RICE AND GRAINS

	KCAL	KJ	GI VALUE
Barley, pearl, boiled	120	510	25 low
Basmati rice, boiled	138	587	58 med
Buckwheat, boiled	364	1522	54 low
Couscous, cooked	227	950	65 med
Egg noodles, boiled	62	264	46 low
Quinoa	309	1311	53 low
Risotto rice, boiled	138	587	69 med
Spaghetti, brown, dried boiled	113	485	37 low

	KCAL	KJ	GI VALUE
Spaghetti, white, boiled	104	442	38 low
White rice, boiled	138	587	98 high

	KCAL	KJ	GI VALUE
Pastry	451	1884	59 med
Pâté, liver	348	1437	0 low
Peaches, canned in juice	39	165	40 low
Peanut/groundnut oil	899	3696	0 low
Peanuts, plain	563	2337	14 low
Peanuts, dry roasted	589	2441	14 low
Pears, canned in juice	33	141	45 low
Pecan nuts	689	2843	10 low
Peeled potatoes, boiled	72	306	101 high
Pepper, black	0	0	0 low
Pepper, chilli	20	83	1 low
Pepper, white	0	0	0 low
Peppers, green, raw	15	65	1 low
Peppers, red, raw	32	134	1 low
Pheasant, meat only roasted	220	918	0 low
Pineapple, canned in juice	47	200	46 low
Pineapple, fresh	41	176	66 med
Pineapple juice, unsweetened	41	177	46 low
Pitta bread, white	255	1084	57 med
Pizza, cheese, thin-crust	277	1168	30 low

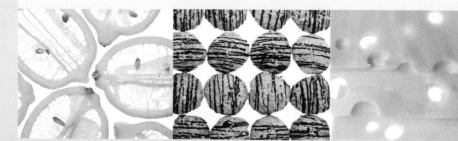

	KCAL	KJ	GI VALUE
Pizza, cheese and tomato, deep-pan	249	1050	36 low
Pizza, cheese and tomato, thin-crust	238	1003	36 low
Plaice, grilled	96	404	0 low
Pork belly, grilled	320	1332	0 low
Pork, chop, lean and fat roasted	301	1256	0 low
Pork, fillet strips, stir-fried	182	764	0 low
Pork, leg, lean, roasted	182	765	0 low
Pork, loin chop, lean grilled	184	774	0 low
Pork, meat only, roasted	182	763	0 low
Pork, steak, lean and fat grilled	198	832	0 low
Porridge oats, dried	401	1698	42 low

POTATOES

	KCAL	KJ	GI VALUE
Baked potato	136	581	85 high
Crisps, potato	530	2215	57 med
Mashed potato, instant	57	245	86 high
New potatoes, canned, reheated and drained	66	281	65 med
New potatoes, unpeeled, boiled in their skins	75	321	76 high
Peeled potatoes, boiled	72	306	101 high
Sweet potatoes, boiled	84	358	46 low

POULTRY AND GAME

	KCAL	KJ	GI VALUE
Chicken, breast, no skin grilled	148	626	0 low
Chicken, drumsticks roasted	185	775	0 low
Chicken, meat and skin roasted	216	912	0 low
Chicken, strips, stir-fried	161	677	0 low
Duck, crispy Chinese	331	1375	0 low
Duck, meat and skin roasted	388	1603	0 low
Duck, meat only, roasted	195	815	0 low
Goose, meat and skin roasted	301	1252	0 low
Pheasant, meat only roasted	220	918	0 low
Rabbit, stewed	114	479	0 low
Turkey, breast, grilled	155	658	0 low
Turkey, meat and skin roasted	171	717	0 low
Turkey, strips, stir-fried	164	692	0 low
Prawns, peeled and boiled	99	418	0 low
Pretzels	381	1596	83 high
Prunes	141	601	29 low

	KCAL	KJ	GI VALUE
Q			
Quinoa	309	1311	53 low
Quorn	86	360	1 low
R			
Rabbit, stewed	114	479	0 low
Radishes	12	49	1 low
Raisins	272	1159	64 med
RICE			
Basmati rice, boiled	138	587	58 med
Risotto rice, boiled	138	587	69 med
Rice cakes, white	374	1591	82 high
Rice cereal, plain	382	1628	82 high
Risotto rice, boiled	138	587	69 med
Rye bread, no grains	219	932	51 low
Rye/pumpernickel bread, with grains	219	932	41 low
S			
Salami	438	1814	0 low
Salmon, canned in oil	153	644	0 low
Salmon, canned in brine	153	644	0 low
Salmon, smoked	142	598	0 low
Salmon, fresh, steamed	194	812	0 low
Salt	0	0	0 low
Sardines, canned in oil	220	918	0 low

	KCAL	KJ	GI VALUE
Sardines, fresh, grilled	195	815	0 low
Sausages, pork, grilled	294	1221	28 low
Scallops, steamed	118	501	0 low
Scones, plain	364	1530	92 high
Sesame oil	899	3696	0 low
Shortbread	509	2133	64 med
Shrimps, canned in brine	94	398	0 low
Shrimps, frozen	73	310	0 low
Skimmed milk	32	136	32 low
SNACKS (SAVOURY)			
Corn chips	459	1927	42 low
Crisps, potato	530	2215	57 med
Peanuts, plain	563	2337	14 low
Peanuts, dry roasted	589	2441	14 low
Pretzels	381	1596	83 high
Rice cakes, white	374	1591	82 high
SNACKS (SWEET)			
Chocolate, milk	520	2177	49 low
Chocolate, plain	510	2137	41 low
Chocolate mousse	149	627	37 low
Chocolate mousse, low-fat	123	518	31 low
Digestive biscuits	465	1956	59 med
Ice cream, full-fat	177	741	61 med
Ice cream, low-fat	119	499	50 low

	KCAL	KJ	GI VALUE
Shortbread	509	2133	64 med
Sponge cake	467	1951	46 low
Yogurt, low-fat	56	237	33 low
Yogurt, low-fat, fruit	78	331	31 low
Yogurt, virtually fat-free, diet	54	230	20 low
Sole fillet, steamed	91	384	0 low
Soy/linseed bread	252	1070	41 low
Soya beans, cooked	141	590	20 low
Soya milk	32	132	36 low
Soya yogurt	72	305	50 low
Spinach, steamed	19	79	1 low
Spinach, raw	25	103	1 low
Split peas, soaked and cooked	126	538	32 low
Sponge cake	467	1951	46 low
Spring greens, steamed	20	82	1 low
Spring greens, raw	33	136	1 low
Spaghetti, brown, dried boiled	113	485	37 low
Spaghetti, white, boiled	104	442	38 low

SPREADS AND DIPS

	KCAL	KJ	GI VALUE
Honey	288	1229	55 low
Hummus	187	781	6 low
Jam, apricot, reduced sugar	123	523	55 low
Jam, strawberry	261	1114	56 med

	KCAL	KJ	GI VALUE
Soy sauce	43	182	1 low
Stilton cheese	410	1698	0 low
Stock cube, chicken	237	990	1 low
Stock cube, vegetable	253	1055	1 low
Stuffing, sage and onion	269	1126	74 high
Sugar	394	1680	68 med
Sultanas	275	1171	56 med
Sunflower oil	899	3696	0 low
Sweetcorn, canned	23	96	46 low
Sweetcorn kernels, boiled	111	470	48 low
Sweetcorn-on-the-cob, boiled	66	280	48 low
Sweet potatoes, boiled	87	372	44 low
Swordfish, grilled	139	583	0 low

T

	KCAL	KJ	GI VALUE
Tea, black	0	0	0 low
Tempeh	166	697	10 low
Tofu, fried	261	1086	1 low
Tofu, steamed	73	304	1 low
Tomato juice, no added sugar	14	62	38 low
Tomato soup, canned	52	219	45 low
Trout fillet, grilled	135	565	0 low
Tuna, canned in brine	99	422	0 low
Tuna, canned in oil	189	794	0 low
Tuna pâté	236	986	0 low

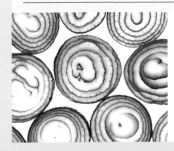
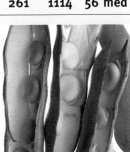

	KCAL	KJ	GI VALUE		KCAL	KJ	GI VALUE
Turkey, breast, grilled	155	658	0 low	**Cauliflower,** boiled	28	117	1 low
Turkey, meat and skin roasted	171	717	0 low	**Cauliflower,** raw	34	142	1 low
				Celery, steamed	8	34	0 low
Turkey, strips, stir-fried	164	692	0 low	**Celery,** raw	7	30	0 low
				Courgette, steamed	19	81	1 low
V				**Courgette,** fried	62	265	1 low
Veal, escalope, fried	196	825	0 low	**Courgette,** raw	18	74	1 low
Veal, escalope, roasted	230	960	0 low	**Cucumber**	10	40	1 low
Veggieburger, grilled	196	821	59 med	**Curly kale,** steamed	24	100	1 low
Vegetable oil	899	3696	0 low	**Curly kale,** raw	33	140	1 low
				Fennel, boiled	11	47	1 low
VEGETABLES				**Fennel,** raw	12	50	1 low
Artichoke, boiled	18	77	1 low	**Green beans,** steamed	25	108	1 low
Artichoke, canned	28	119	1 low	**Green beans,** raw	24	99	1 low
Asparagus, steamed	26	110	1 low	**Leeks,** steamed	21	87	1 low
Aubergine, fried	302	1246	1 low	**Lettuce,** round	14	59	1 low
Avocado	190	784	1 low	**Lettuce,** iceberg	13	53	1 low
Bean sprouts, raw	31	131	1 low	**Mangetout,** steamed	26	111	1 low
Bean sprouts, stir-fried	72	298	1 low	**Mangetout,** raw	32	136	1 low
				Mangetout, stir-fried	71	298	1 low
Beetroot, boiled	36	154	64 med	**Marrow,** boiled	9	38	1 low
Broccoli, green, steamed	24	100	1 low	**Mushrooms,** fried	157	645	1 low
Broccoli, green, raw	33	138	1 low	**Mushrooms,** raw	13	55	1 low
Brussels sprouts, steamed	35	153	1 low	**Mustard and cress**	13	56	1 low
Cabbage, steamed	16	67	1 low	**Okra,** boiled	28	119	1 low
Cabbage, raw	26	109	1 low	**Okra,** fried	269	1122	1 low
Carrots, steamed	24	100	31 low	**Onions,** fried	164	684	0 low
Carrots, raw	35	146	49 low				

	KCAL	KJ	GI VALUE		KCAL	KJ	GI VALUE
Onions, raw	36	150	0 low	**Wheat cereal**	89	376	0 low
Pepper, chilli	20	83	1 low	**Whelks**	137	576	0 low
Peppers, green, raw	15	65	1 low	**White bread**	235	1002	70 high
Peppers, red, raw	32	134	1 low	**White rice,** cooked	138	587	98 high
Radishes	12	49	1 low	**Whiting,** steamed	92	406	0 low
Spinach, steamed	19	79	1 low	**Whole milk**	66	274	31 low
Spinach, raw	25	103	1 low	**Wholemeal bread**	217	922	77 high
Spring greens, steamed	20	82	1 low	**Worcestershire sauce**	65	276	1 low
Spring greens, raw	33	136	1 low				
Sweetcorn, canned	23	96	46 low	Y			
Sweetcorn-on-the-cob, boiled	66	280	48 low	**Yam,** boiled	133	568	37 low
				Yeast extract	180	763	0 low
Sweet potatoes, boiled	84	358	46 low	**Yogurt,** low-fat	56	237	33 low
Tomato juice, no added sugar	14	62	38 low	**Yogurt,** low-fat, fruit	78	331	31 low
Watercress	22	94	1 low	**Yogurt,** virtually fat-free, diet	54	230	20 low
Yam, boiled	133	568	37 low				
Venison, roasted	165	698	0 low				
Vinegar	22	89	0 low				
W							
Waffles	334	1401	76 high				
Water	0	0	0 low				
Water biscuits	440	1859	77 high				
Watercress	22	94	1 low				
Watermelon, no skin	31	133	72 high				
Weetabix	352	1498	69 med				

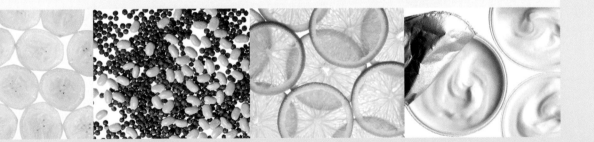

Index

Acknowledgements

Executive editor: Nicola Hill
Project editor: Alice Bowden
Deputy creative director: Geoff Fennell
Designer: Ginny Zeal

Photography: Will Heap, Mike Prior, Ian O'Leary, Gareth Sambidge
Home economist: Sara Lewis
Senior production controller: Martin Croshaw